Pyrography for Beginners Handbook

Learn to Burn Guide in Wood Burning with Starter Projects and Patterns

Stephen Fleming

© Copyright 2020 - All rights reserved.

The content contained within this book may not be reproduced, duplicated, or transmitted without direct written permission from the author or the publisher.

Under no circumstances will any blame or legal responsibility be held against the publisher, or author, for any damages, reparation, or monetary loss due to the information contained within this book. Either directly or indirectly.

Legal Notice:

This book is copyright protected. This book is only for personal use. You cannot amend, distribute, sell, use, quote or paraphrase any part, or the content within this book, without the consent of the author or publisher.

Disclaimer Notice:

Please note the information contained within this document is for educational and entertainment purposes only. All effort has been executed to present accurate, up to date, and reliable, complete information. No warranties of any kind are declared or implied. Readers acknowledge that the author is not engaging in the rendering of legal, financial, medical, or professional advice. The content within this book has been derived from various sources. Please consult a licensed professional before attempting any techniques outlined in this book.

By reading this document, the reader agrees that under no circumstances are the author responsible for any losses, direct or indirect, which are incurred as a result of the use of the information contained within this document, including, but not limited to, —errors, omissions, or inaccuracies.

Bonus Booklet- DIY Series

Thanks for purchasing the book. In addition to the content, we are also providing an additional booklet consisting of Monthly planner and Project Schedule template for your initial projects.

Also, it has a few evergreen patterns for your practice.

Download the booklet by typing the below link.

(* Note: This booklet is common for wood and leather crafts)

http://bit.ly/leatherbonus

Cheers!

Copyright © 2020 Stephen Fleming

All rights reserved.

Table of Contents

#	Chapter Name	Page No.
1	Introduction to Pyrography	7-24
2	Pyrography Tools	25-38
3	Designing, Tracing, and Shading	39-61
4	Coloring, Polishing, and Finishing	62-64
5	Safety and Health Concerns	65-68
6	Starter Projects in Pyrography	69-89
7	FAQ's From Practitioners	90-96
8	Some Sample Designs and Patterns	97-103

PREFACE

This is the second book in my DIY series after the _Leatherworking Starter Handbook._

Of all the crafts I've done, Pyrography offers the most value for money. It gives me immense satisfaction and serves my creative purposes for practicing art on the weekends.

The best part is this art provides something inspiring, imaginative, and empowering for everyone.

If you're a beginner, get a scrap wood and use your existing soldering pen to start the artwork. Later, you can shift to a proper burner. If you like calligraphy, you can burn letters. A friend of mine is a space enthusiast, and he's making spaceships!

With experience, you can also master the art of shading, which gives depth to any artwork. Drawing hair, fur, or skin of an animal takes time, but it's worthwhile to put the effort. The best part of this skill is that it makes one of the best, personalized presents for the loved ones. As the art ages with time, it leaves a memorable piece of history to the future generation.

This isn't a traditional book but an effort from your friend to present the experience and discussions while learning this art in the last few years (4 years to be precise). I'm not an expert (there are many we know who are just fabulous and doing it for more than 10 years) but only a passionate, dedicated learner improving with each project.

But more importantly, if you're merely starting, I can provide you the exact practical information you're seeking because the **best person to guide you is the one just a few steps ahead of you**!

Finally, I've included realistic photographs, discussions, and tips received my journey in Pyrography over the years. Also, one chapter is dedicated explicitly to safety measures while burning as it's of the utmost importance.

Cheers, and let's start the transformative journey!

Stephen Fleming

Some Words of Wisdom from Pyrography Practitioners

- As a beginner, I initially had the misconception that if I pushed harder into the wood, it'd make a darker burn. That's totally false!
- The best advice given to me has been to glide over the wood with the tip. Earlier, I was adding too much pressure and was digging into the wood as I burned in my picture.
- Also, make sure before you start to sand, sand, and sand the wood!
- Before burning the cutting board, make sure there isn't a stain on it because it can be toxic to burn over the stain.
- Spend some time each day working on your art. Practice regularly.
- Type of burner depends on how you like to hold your burner. If you don't mind being 3-4 inches away from your wood, then a Walnut Hollow Versa tool is useful; but if you want to hold the pen like you would a pencil, then you may use * Optima I burner/Razertip(* Different models of burners burning pen).
- I've learned to use the shading tool at a low temperature and go lightly over the wood in layers.
- For tracing the diagram on the wood, use graphite paper since it's easier to erase if you make a mistake.
- Make sure when you trace it on, use a light hand. Remember to let the tool do the work and don't press too hard.
- This hobby isn't cheap. When you get a pen, you'll need wood pieces, sanding device/tool/pads for the best result of burning, and then you require a coating or vanish substance to protect the pieces 'you've done. The next thing is how and where to sell them. You might think that you'll merely do this hobby for giving away as gifts or charity, but when you reach the point that there are so many burnt pieces at your house, you might think about how to sell them.
- But one thing that you have to be sure is you love the craft. Then only investing in tools and wood would be fruitful.

1. Introduction to Pyrography

What's Pyrography? Brief History and Introduction

Definition as per Wikipedia: (Refer: https://en.wikipedia.org/wiki/Pyrography)

"Pyrography or pyrogravure is the freehanded art of decorating wood or other materials with burn marks resulting from the controlled application of a heated object such as a poker. It's also known as pokerwork or wood burning. The term means "writing with fire," from the Greek pur (fire) and graphos (writing)."

Below is one of the oldest Pyrography images:

Brunhilde Asleep, 1902, Reference: Margaret Fernie Eaton [Public domain]

Pyrography is an art of burning of sketches or drawings right into the timber. Color is often added with oil pencils after the burning is completed, but it's typically maintained to a minimum. Although some skill is needed, great art pieces are mostly made with practice, and also one will certainly learn their own style and tool with time.

The ancient people began to create their wood-burning tools as they progressed. The first tool was made of portable pots with holes. Pokers were inserted in the holes. The pioneers used the pokers to burn the wood. It was a dangerous and challenging tool to use. Hence, wood-burning was limited to only those who knew how to operate it. During medieval times, the people discovered that when they heated metal objects, they could use it to burn and design the woods. They first used it to design simple objects in their homes, like wooden spoons and bowls. It became an excellent hobby for many rich people. Some people from medieval times, especially blacksmiths, then made it into commercial art.

Commercial opportunities from the upgraded wood burning tools:

Aside from making swords and armors, they also began decorating containers and chests with intricate Pyrography designs. The modern wood burner used today was only discovered during the early 20th century. The tool was initially used to solder metals. It was easier to fuse metal using an electronic solder than doing it manually. However, wood burning craftsmen discovered that they could also use the same instrument to draw wood designs better. The tool was smaller and was easier to control than the traditional pokers they used. As a result, manufacturers of metal solders soon included different points, sizes, and nibs to increase the variety and possibility of designs. The discovery of the new tool gave ordinary people a chance to learn wood burning in a faster, easier, and safer way.

The interest in wood-burning increased, especially in Asian and European countries, because of this advancement. Chinese and European creators would mark or personalize their chests and leather bags through Pyrography. In recent years, the interest in wood-burning had significantly increased. Wood burning machines have also advanced, and companies can now mass-produce wood burning crafts at a lower price. But, the advancement of wood-burning devices doesn't stop the interest of hobbyists and artists who want to have hand-made wood burning decorations with rich, intricate, and original designs.

The threats involved with Pyrography are mentioned below:

- Burning self with the iron
- Burning anything else that ought to not be burnt (a lot of pencil design irons has no "off "button with the iron, as well as no "on" sign lamp)
- Getting sawdust into the eyes.
- Improperly using wood and asphyxiating one's self.

The equipment and also materials we'll be utilizing consist of:

- A pyrographer's iron(Solid point Burner, Wire Nib Burner or Laser Burner)
- A steel stand for the iron
- A basic multi-faced tip for the iron (as you become skilled, you can add specialized tips)
- Some sandpaper (150-180 great grit, so a light sanding is needed, 80-100 tool grit if some ridges require eliminated from the wood). It's best to wear some eye security when doing any sanding of timber.
- Some carbon paper may be available in helpful in addition to a sketchpad, and mapping paper is handy as well
- A well-ventilated job location.
- Wood

- Some oil-based tinted pencils

Steps for Pyrography

Below are the sequential actions for completing a Pyrography project.

Prep work.

The first step is to prepare the timber for a clean and even burn. If the Basswood is a bit harsh, take some 80-100 grit sandpaper to it (utilize a fine sand block to keep it even). If the timber isn't extremely bumpy, review it with the 150-180 grit sandpaper to obtain a smooth surface.

This is where you require the shatterproof glass or goggles to avoid obtaining splinters of wood in your eye(s). Blow off the dust. Next, we need an illustration or sketch.

The Sketch

Sketch up whatever you want to burn onto the timber on some tracing paper. It isn't required to make it overly outlined at this moment; however, if you wish to include the details for yourself while burning, proceed. As soon as this is completed, position the carbon paper on the timber (put the carbon side down), and the tracing you did over it as you want it to appear on the timber (as you improve with the iron or if you have the ability to make decent sketches straight onto the wood, these steps can be avoided). Backtrace the diagram (major lines) so that a light carbon copy is drawn on the wood.

Draw it directly   **Trace it using carbon paper**

Action 3: Fire up the Iron

Now, after doing away with the carbon paper (some of it can be a little bit exhausting), we prepare to start the next step: If you haven't positioned your iron on the "stand" and connected it in yet, please do so. Wait a couple of minutes while it warms up. If you have a scrap item of timber close by, you can occasionally examine it by holding the tip to the wood momentarily. If it burns immediately, then it implies that the iron is ready.

Grasp the iron strongly, much like a pencil is held. Don't "suffocate" your iron. It'll undoubtedly make it harder to burn correctly, and also ultimately, you'll "feel the heat" of the iron. The picture should offer a close estimate of how to hold the iron "a lot of the moment." There will be times you'll have altered the grasp to obtain the effect you want.

Wood Burning Kit

Action 4: Getting a Real Start into Pyrography

In the beginning ensure to gently "glide" the pen, as well as not try to "push it" (some people like to burn from the top to down, others like to center out; whereas I like to do the overview first and then decide which way to follow). Our tip offers many usages: a point, for fine work, a "blade side" for the sketch, and a level side for area burning; that is, for burning or shading a bigger area each time.

Begin gradually yet not too sluggishly (it's best to do a little bit of practicing on smaller sized, less costly items of wood) maintaining your "speed" or holding your iron consistently.

You'll certainly realize that there's much too either draw towards yourself or from side to side; everyone seems to have their preference (although you might need to do both at times). Turning the wood is far better than attempting to "push" the iron. Complete the outline and the major parts of the drawing/carbon image and then take a couple of minutes to look at it. It is like the monitoring of the structure.

Simple Wood Burning – Honeybee   **Coloring Wood**

Yet also bear in mind, sometimes way too much detail can spoil an otherwise fantastic item.

You'll soon discover with practice when to stop (possibly after spending several hours on an item, and afterward placing one "last" touch, ruins the entire point - it happens to the best pyrographers, so it'll most definitely happen to you as well).

Action 5: Completing the spaces/gaps

Shading, filling up, and also too much information must also be prevented when just beginning to discover this art form. As you improve later, you'll wish to "feather," shade, add depth, and also add many various other details. There are special tips out there to assist with these works.

Shading Technique

However, these aren't initially required. The one tip I've used more of than any is the detailing tip. It wears down quickly and soon you're virtually shading without any tip at all.

Step 6: Maintain clean tools

Some recommendations: If the tip gets too stained, it definitely won't heat up well. However, extreme cleaning of tips wears them down much quicker.

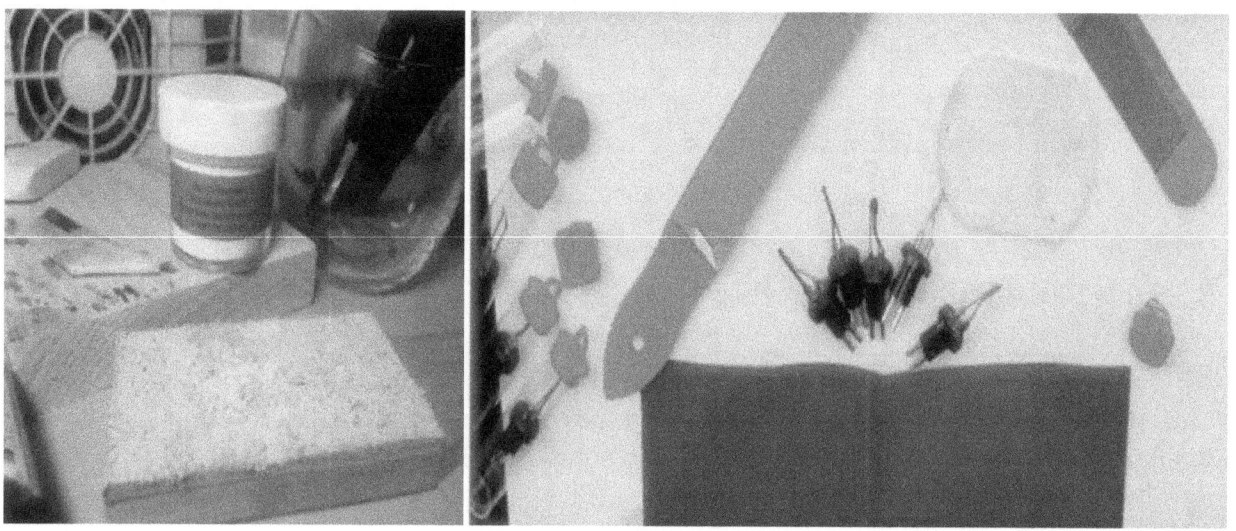

Sandpaper for Tip Cleaning   **Cleaning cloth, sponge, and sandpaper**

Maintain a moist sponge nearby, preferably one that's "anchored" in some way so that you can draw the tip across it from time to time. It effectively cleans the carbon build-up without the demand to sanding away the copper tip. Remember, the iron is hot, so it doesn't just burn timber, yet skin is specifically at risk of burns. Keep the iron's tip off the wood until you desire it to be melting. Raise it, relocate, and glide it as quickly as you can without rushing.

Wood Selection for Pyrography

We'll discuss at the most effective kinds of wood for burning, and we'll be utilizing two burners on the wood kind, so you can see how each one burns through the wood.

Basswood is the first wood we'll examine. It's one of the best woods for burning. It's soft and easy to burn with practically no grains. It has a strong surface area of soft burning wood, and it's gorgeous. You can see right here just how easily the burner burns through the wood.

Basswood

Birchwood burns much like Basswood; the grains are regularly soft, and you can discover this in the big box stores much like Basswood; you can see in the below picture exactly how the burners move through the wood grains easily.

The next wood is **Oak**. It's a little trickier; it's hard as well as the grains are inconsistent; the darker grains are softer as well as the lighter grains are harder. As I swiftly drag my burner down the strip of oak, you can see the inconsistency in the burn lines. That's the distinction of the grains as I burn a much deeper and slower line; you can see the moisture creating an untidy side.

Plus, oak is among the much more pricey woods to get in the shops. The next wood we'll be checking out is **Poplar** is my absolute favorite as well as one of the best beginner woods in my point of view for three reasons: it's super easy to burn, really obtainable, and allows you to specifically tailor the dimension of the wood canvas you want to burn.

The grains are softer on the boards, which makes a stable wood-burning surface. You can burn easily and observe the wood burner moving quickly through the wood.

Birchwood

Oak Wood

This next wood we'll cover is **Yellow Pine**. Yellow pine is challenging because the grains aren't favorable for burning. You can see below the inconsistent burn line and also as I promptly move the burner throughout the wood. The lighter grain is soft, while the darker one is really hard. Yellow pine is utilized very often in wood-burning art; it's affordable and also just one of the most convenient woods to get. Like oak, there's a lot of wetness that bubbles out when burning. Total yellow pine is among my least preferred woods to burn because of the disparity, as well as the grains and the dampness that bubbles out.

Poplar

Yellow Pine

It makes for a low-quality burn and a finished item.

The last wood we'll examine is **White Pine**. I like it over the yellow pine as the grains are much more consistent. You can see the lines in the below photo that is smooth and even. We generally burn white pine and palate wood together. Use caution when burning pallet wood, since there are some safety precautions to follow, so do a little bit of study before you start burning any combination woods.

White Pine

A sample project work

Is Wood Burning Easy For Beginners?

Wood burning is among those rare hobbies that are cheap, simple to enter into, and also one where you can achieve astonishing results in merely a few days.

Just how very easy, you ask?

I never did any crafting earlier. I started with leather crafting and took up Pyrography after that. I engaged in leather burning first and later began enjoying wood burning.

If you already have a soldering iron, after that, you don't even have to buy the additional one for timber burning. Just don't use your most excellent soldering tip, and you're good to go. You'll undoubtedly require some wood. If you intend to use natural wood, then you'll need to sand it first.

Or else, the surface will be harsh and you'll have a tough time trying to make decent forms. The most useful thing you can do is to acquire a piece of plywood and then cut it up right into smaller areas.

Plywood is truly smooth with a beautiful texture, as well as is perfect for timber burning, and most importantly, no sanding is required. (For safety reasons since plywood is human-made wood, burn in a well-ventilated area with safety gears).

Circles   **Different Tips**

You'll additionally require an item of fining sandpaper, in the quantity of 300 to 400 grit.

When the wood burns away, soot begins to gather on the tip. This can leave marks and also decrease the heating result. Therefore, it's a good practice to clean the tip often.

Finally, don't forget about your health. Breathing in smoke is never healthy, so ensure you have some proper ventilation in place. For example, I'm using my 3D printed fume extractor.

That's, in fact, all you need to begin, so let's go! You need to spend the very first few minutes with your new device.

Try making straight lines, circles, sharp lines, and a little bit of shading. See what happens if you weigh down harder. Play around up until you get a feel for it. It's much easier when your hand stays in the very same setting as well as when you move the work item instead.

Now you might be wondering what's next.

Unless you're one of those gifted people who can draw, you'll need to make use of some pattern transferring technique.

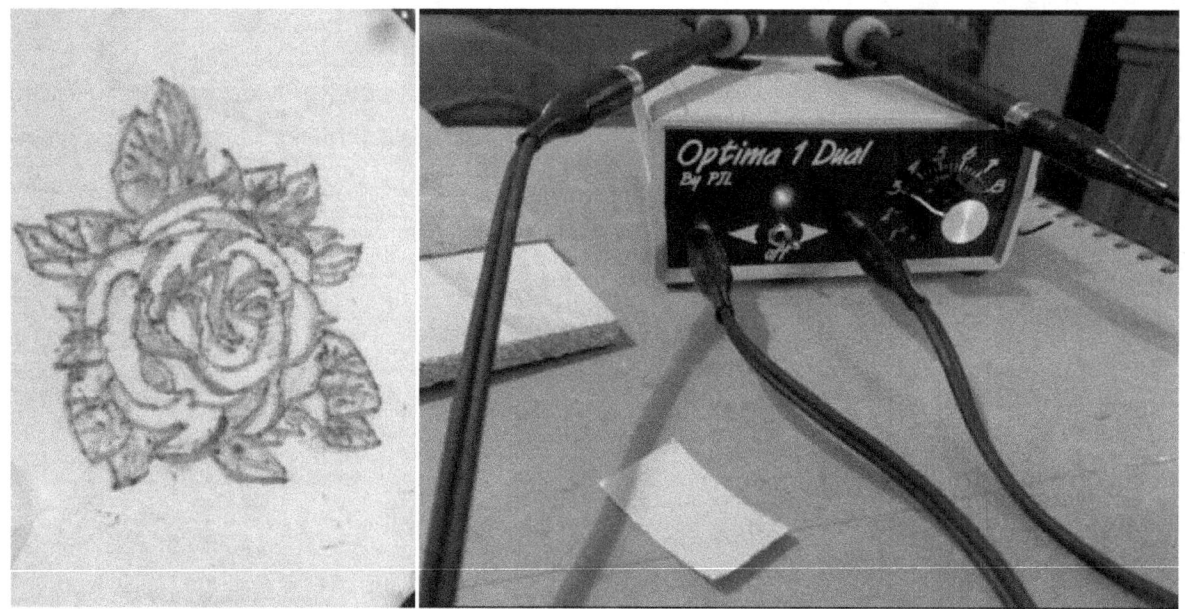

Sample First Project and Soldering Rod

You can check a lot of different methods online, but they're either untidy, don't function well, or you have to play around with chemicals. By far, the most effective as well as the easiest technique is utilizing an inkjet printer.

If you make use of an empty sheet of sticker label paper, you can print straight on it.

The surface is smooth as well as plastic-like, so anything you print doesn't get soaked up by it. This is best for transferring the image. Very carefully place the paper in place, hold it down and, after that, utilize some edge to transfer the picture.

Do a fast clean-up, and you can make use of the very same paper over again. Ok, now comes the simple part - tracing the image. Begin with the sides first and afterward fills it in later.

Attempt to be as consistent with your speed as well as pressure. Once the outline is done, you can proceed to fill it in accordingly. I've experienced that making small circles, rather than lines, gives you far better results.

You have extra control over how much it sheds as well as the surface needs to wind up looking smoother. In case you have a 3D printer, you can make any stencils you desire. As soon as you obtain some technique, you're ready to proceed to shade. Shading is tricky because it's common to overdo it.

Example of Fume Extractor

Simply keep practicing, and it'll look better every time you do it. Before we transition to the last step, please remember that you can combine your work with paint, too. If you're currently acquainted with calligraphy, you can utilize the very same abilities with wood burning, too.

The only difference is that as opposed to lowering on the pen, you must slow down, which will enhance the size of the line. If you haven't done calligraphy in the past, why not give it a try?

Pyrography Tips for Beginners:

1. **Keep Tools Clean**: I use a tea strainer to keep my Pyrography pen tidy. If you rub on it, it'll certainly remove the carbon. Keeping the burning pen clean is very important to be safe and also for making sharp lines.

2. **Find your favorite tip and use it for all activities**:

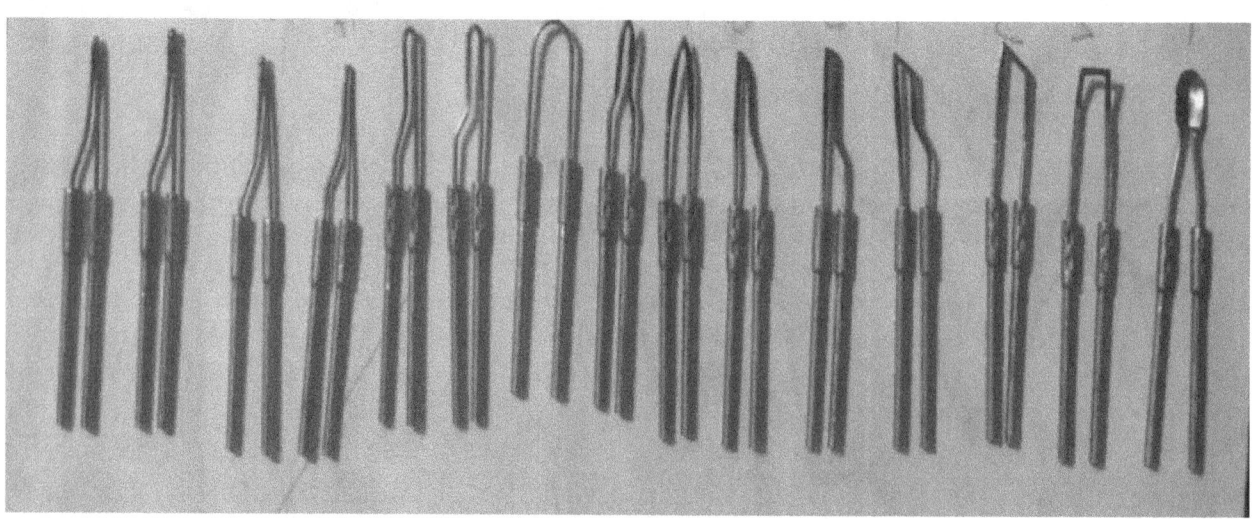

I'd also suggest discovering every technique with just one tip. If you wish to try and also discover exactly how to:
- Shade with that tip
- Detailing with that tip
- Create large and small dark and light areas

By doing this, you'll actually save a lot of time from not needing to alter your tips waiting on it to cool down all these things. Also, you'll additionally trigger fewer damages to your tips if you're taking off with pliers to avoid yourself from burning. You may likewise harm your tool. You may damage the element inside frequently changing tips back and forth. So this tip can help you learn fast because you would be trying many things with this one tip (The old fashioned way of specializing one tool first!).

3. **Use a black-and-white image**: It makes the whole process so much less complicated. When you're using a color image, it's difficult to tell with the various tones and with the highlights the darks will be. If you transform that to monotone, it's a lot easier to see that because burning is going to be monotone tuned. So it's going to be much easier to use a black and white photo for perfect shading of the project.

4. **Usage of top-notch/quality products for gallery work**: You can start with any wood, but if you intend to sell or showcase your project, use a decent piece of wood. I don't know how many times I've seen incredible outstanding like art like Pyrography items done on cheap timber or simply bad timber. For example, I've observed this incredible art done on plywood, and you recognize plywood is cheap. The selection of the wood is also very important. I further have realized that pinewood isn't that great for wood burning. If you plan to sell your craft, then I suggest you use three-inch-thick wood you can get online for 30 to 60 dollars. It's worth the investment if you're planning to take it to the gallery or sell it.
So, my advice would be to start with plywood or a cheaper piece of wood, but once doing it seriously and want to showcase your project, use a better one.

5. **Use High Contrast Photo**: This helps to give the photo more depth. Suppose you have a photo on iPad you'd like to make on wood, but the contrast is less, and there's no depth in it. When your darks are dark and your lights are light, that really gives your overall picture a lot of depth, which is what I try to do and every single piece.

Details of Pyrography Pen/Burner Tips and Their Usages

Tools that Rule: Pen/Burner Tips:

Burner/Pen tips differ merely in terms of how they're created and the targeted burning activity they have to perform. Every type of pen is unique with respect to kind of burn, width, as well as tone it'll produce when used for Pyrography. For example, both the round tips, as well as loop pens, generate dark and also noticeable lines; in contrast, the rounded shader or thin-edged spear tip will offer you deeper, slimmer lines. As a starter, the set of tips useful for you are:

- Flat spoon-shaped shader
- A tight curved loop creating tip
- Curved-edged spear shader
- Ballpoint composing tip
- Wide-wire square tip shader

Tips of these kinds will work for any type of project you might want to take up as a novice. As you progress with this craft and also end up much more skilled in your art, you can utilize expert tips. Tips can be found in different dimensions, names, and forms. This difference depends upon the specific supplier for your devices. Some pens have the tip completely fixed, while others can be changed.

For example, when using the pens with permanent tips, the cable for burning is joined together with the pen and cannot be put away in any manner. On the other hand, pens with tips can be changed to achieve various tips, so take full, creative advantage with the pen. Some brand names of pens are constructed to function distinctively with the electrical makeup of that specific Pyrography device.

You may, nonetheless, encounter makers that allow the user to take advantage of pens from other brands on their devices. This isn't recommended as your system might malfunction. In buying a new unit, take careful consideration of the functional designs of the pen, the power ranking, the connection in between the unit and the pen, and also other features that'll certainly enable you to obtain a smooth burning experience.

Specifically, the ball tipped pens are available in diverse sizes; the smaller diameter tipped is used for building and constructing slim lines, as well as the pens with a larger size, which are best for the development of more substantial, thicker lines. The primary objectives for this type of pen are to deal with the filling, scrubbing, and also shading.

The Fine Lines: Creating & Detailing

The pattern can be added to your job to make it much more eye-catching. A temperature level on the pen can be used to create the lines, and then you can proceed to burn your desired style gently.

After you're through with the shading, repeat the lines once again, but this time using higher temperatures. Don't just burn one line width but change the density to make your project a lot more diverse and intricate.

Fill to Thrill: Fill Up Texturing

To develop a strong filling in the artwork, a high or medium temperature setup will suffice, in addition to utilizing a ball-tipped pen.

Closely filling the dots with each other will definitely make space show up in a darker tone. A tool temperature level setup is more desirable than a higher temperature level setting, as it can cause dot spilling.

TripleS: The Scrubby Shading Strategy (SSS)

The ball tipped pen can be utilized in developing short as well as small scrubby strokes to create a similarly dispersed shading .

To produce, crubby shading, start a well-regulated burn with side to side movement with your hands for fairly straight lines. You can likewise develop semi-circular, closely collaborated lines. The lines need to be firmly packed together in different layers to provide a dark tone to that specific space.

Strike Right: Striking Lines Formation

The temperature level setup for this burn is not that important. All you need to do is to keep the tip of the pen straight on the real wood surface. With this, you can create the desired lines. If you use a low temperature, the lines will appear in light tones; and with a higher temperature setting, the lines will come out dark.

Pattern Pizazz: Appearance Patterns

With the loop creating tip, you can create any structure pattern you want. Hatched out patterns, curls, rounded lines, and circles are perfect kinds of structures to form with the loop writing tip. To make the tonal value light, your lines shouldn't be compact; and if you want the area to appear darker, then the lines should be dense.

Flat Off the Bat: The Flat Spear Shader

This burning tip has a pointed or rounded tip with a flat surface. It likewise has a curved tip, so it's referred to as a spoon shader. To work with this type successfully, you need to establish the temperature level at the highest possible point due to the thick steel tip. In scrubby shading with this tip, the flat side of the pen ought to straighten with the solid wood while you draw fast brief lines. The shader can be pulled up a little with the tip to move quickly in creating rounded shading activities.

The Curved-Edge Spear Shader

The spear shader has a bulkier tip than the curved-edge spear shader; thus, it can offer thicker as well as dark lines without a higher temperature setting. You also get to produce a light, slight burn without the development of a dark tip on the work surface, unlike when using the ball tipped pen. With the framework of the tip, the formation of long shading strokes can be created. You position the tip against the surface area and also pull gradually as the tones are created.

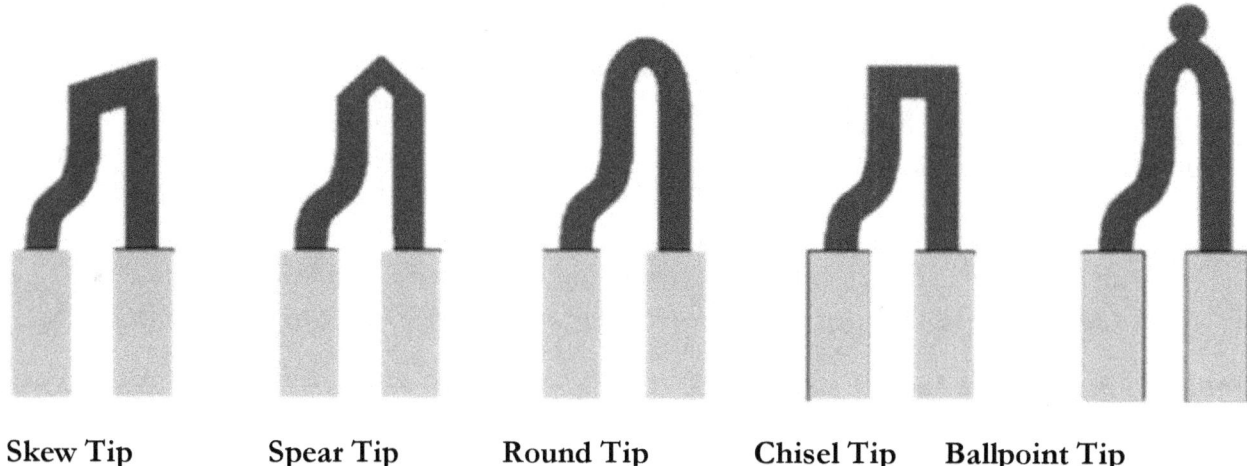

Skew Tip **Spear Tip** **Round Tip** **Chisel Tip** **Ballpoint Tip**

The Wide-Wire Square Shader

This is the tip that both newbie's and also specialists need to have in the toolkit. The framework of the tip makes it able to color with thick feeds quicker. If you're servicing a large piece of art that calls for a lot of shading and also filling up, this tip will certainly assist you to get it done in a few minutes rather than investing the whole day on the job. In some machines, you'll find that the pen has parts that have been produced to be fitted with nibs that are customized from Nichrome. To make the nibs safe into the holding components, a screw can be used. As you become more efficient in this art, you can look to develop your special nib if you do not want to go with what the manufacturers have to offer. The Nichrome cable can be bent right into any shape you desire to as the project available needs. You can make the nib either little or thick to make light burns or thick and darker burns.

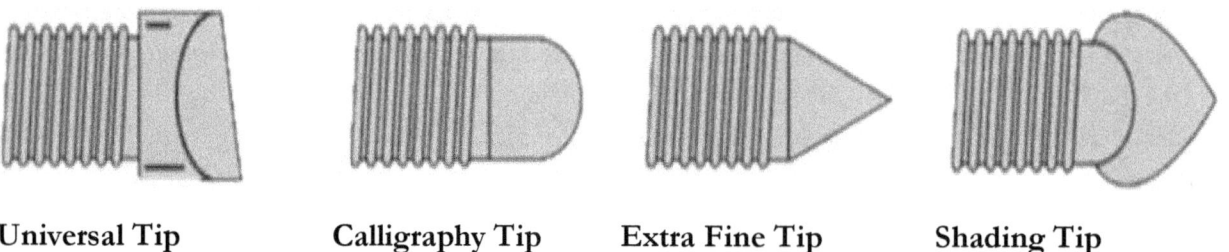

Universal Tip **Calligraphy Tip** **Extra Fine Tip** **Shading Tip**

2. Pyrography Tools

Below are the raw materials and tools necessary for practicing the art of Pyrography.

1. Wood

There's one essential material in Pyrography, without which, you can't practice this craft. That relevant product is wood. You can make designs on any softwood; however, crafters prefer the following wood for their durability:

These are:

1. **Pine**: It's the least expensive amongst the woods preferred by professionals. It has several grains and also knots that make it a bit challenging to use for beginners. It takes much effort to create designs that require lines with a consistent width.

2. **Birch**: It isn't as affordable as pine. However, it's the preferred wood for beginners to practice. The wood has a smooth surface and burns lighter than other woods. You can make modifications quickly.

3. **Basswood:** This sort of wood is the leading choice for numerous wood-burning professionals. It's light with also grains and knots. It melts conveniently and also it also has color. Thus, it's much easier to make.

4. **Bamboo:** Bamboo is additionally ending up being a preferred base for wood burning projects. It's less costly, as well as smooth.

5. Any kind of **hardwood:** Hardwood such as elm and also oak are likewise excellent for wood burning. Clean or ready hardwoods are expensive since they are tough to prepare. However, they have a smoother surface area than the softwoods discussed over. Oak and elm are often used by those with advanced woodworkers. However, their tip or smaller branches are softer than the primary branches and also trunk. You can utilize them for tiny decorations, such as Christmas tree ornaments, pendants, or various other devices.

6. **Gourd:** This isn't real wood, yet a dry gourd has a wonderful texture for wood burning. It's cheaper and also suitable for practicing your strokes. Nonetheless, placing an actual design on a gourd might require some techniques.

7. **Cedar timber**: It's additional softwood, and also grains aren't a huge fear. Line art will bulge perfectly, but gradient shadings will barely be discovered.

8. **Cherry timber**: It delivers terrific aromas while you function! I only tried this one recently, but it also seemed great.

Never burn wood that has some finishing. The burning of varnish isn't good for health and wellness, and could also make the wood burst into tiny fires. Also, don't use MDF wood.

2. The Wood Burner

One more crucial device in Pyrography that newbie requires is the Wood Burner.

It's a tool that provides a consistent temperature level and tip for beginner wood burning. Many wood burners come with a **Universal Tip**, which imitates a pen.

It isn't advisable for a newbie, according to some experts. Beginners would find it difficult to control due to the fact that it has a broader point. Experts recommend that novices ought to initially master these 3 points or nibs, prior to making use of the universal tip.

Little spherical tip: The tip is as huge as the ballpoint pen. Use it to make elaborate details on your wood. You can use it to practice your strokes.

Large spherical tip: The tip is larger and creates a thicker line than the universal point. Nevertheless, it's much easier to manage. Utilize it to draw thicker lines as well as harsh woods.

Shading tip: This tip remains in the shape of a spade. You can use it to burn slim layers at the background for shading results.

Fine tip: This tip resembles the little point pen; however, it has a sharper line. It's thinner as well as great for dual lining or for adding details.

The Razer Tip Wood Burner Pen: There's an additional type of wood burner in the market called the razer tip. It's preferred for the novice as well as expert wood burner designers.

The tip is made from a versatile wire. You can draw nearly all the strokes and also designs with it. However, some of its attributes are better for those with experience.

The Branding Tips: You can purchase branding tips if you're serious about wood burning. Manufacturers have pre-made tips, such as letters, blossom designs, and also geometric styles. Some also approve the order for personalized tips.

Various Other Products and Devices for Finishing

Sandpaper: It has two major uses. It's used to clean up some tiny wood fibers on the surface of your wood as well as to clean the tip of your wood burners. There are circumstances that you also require it to eliminate some burnt part, as well as fine sandpaper, can do the task.

Masking Tape or Artist's Tape: It isn't a required device in Pyrography, yet it works to cover the parts you don't wish to burn. It's excellent when you want to put margins in your borders. If you're collaborating with a lightweight wood or small-sized wood, you can additionally make use of the tape to hold back the wood for far better stability. It's made from paper and also doesn't leave any marks on the wood.

Graphite Paper: You use graphite paper to trace your drawing on your wood. It's preferable than carbon paper due to the fact that you can simply remove the lines with the common gray-and-white eraser. Lines made over carbon documents are darker and might need to erased/ sand away to remove it.

Nonfusible Interfacing: This product is useful when you're designing vases or other rounded woods. It'll certainly help keep your graphite paper still in the rounded areas while you map your layouts. You can locate this cellular lining in textile stores.

Gray-and- White Pencil Eraser: This ordinary and also inexpensive pencil eraser comes useful when you're designing your theme and moving it on the wood. You can remove the graphite lines using the gray portion of the eraser after you have burned your wood. Don't overlook the white eraser. It assists you in cleaning up the surface of your wood without ruining the designs.

Spots and Wax Based Oil Pencils

These are used to make your layouts stand out. You can provide your task an antique wood appearance with the gel pens or make it vivid utilizing wax-based oil pencils.

Steel Rules: These are chosen over plastic rulers so that they can help you in two ways. You can use it for creating your layout, and you can utilize them to burn straight lines straight on your wood.

Metal Themes: There are steel themes for alphabets, basic shapes as well as various other typical drawings. You can equip on those as well as utilize it for doing easy and simple styles on your wood.

Printer: A Laser Printer will certainly help you transfer a printed layout much faster with the help of details transferring wood burner device or iron.

Using a Wood Burner

Wood burner packages commonly consist of guides as well as handbooks on just how to use your wood burner tips; however, most of them don't tell you when it is the correct time to utilize your while you work. Below are the straightforward steps on how to use your wood burner appropriately:

1. Disconnect your wood burner. Even if your wood burner has a switch, you must unplug it

for your safety and security.
2. Place your tip on your wood burner before plugging it.
3. Place it on its stand and wait on at the very least 5 minutes before using it on your wood.
4. Don't push the tip to make darker lines. Just allow your tip to remain in the very same area for a long time before relocating to an additional spot. If you press the tip hard, it could flex as well as damage it. Just position it lightly on the board and also let the heat work.
5. When you're done with your work, return the wood burner right into its stand and also unplug it. Let it cool off completely before removing the tip and returning it to the toolbox.

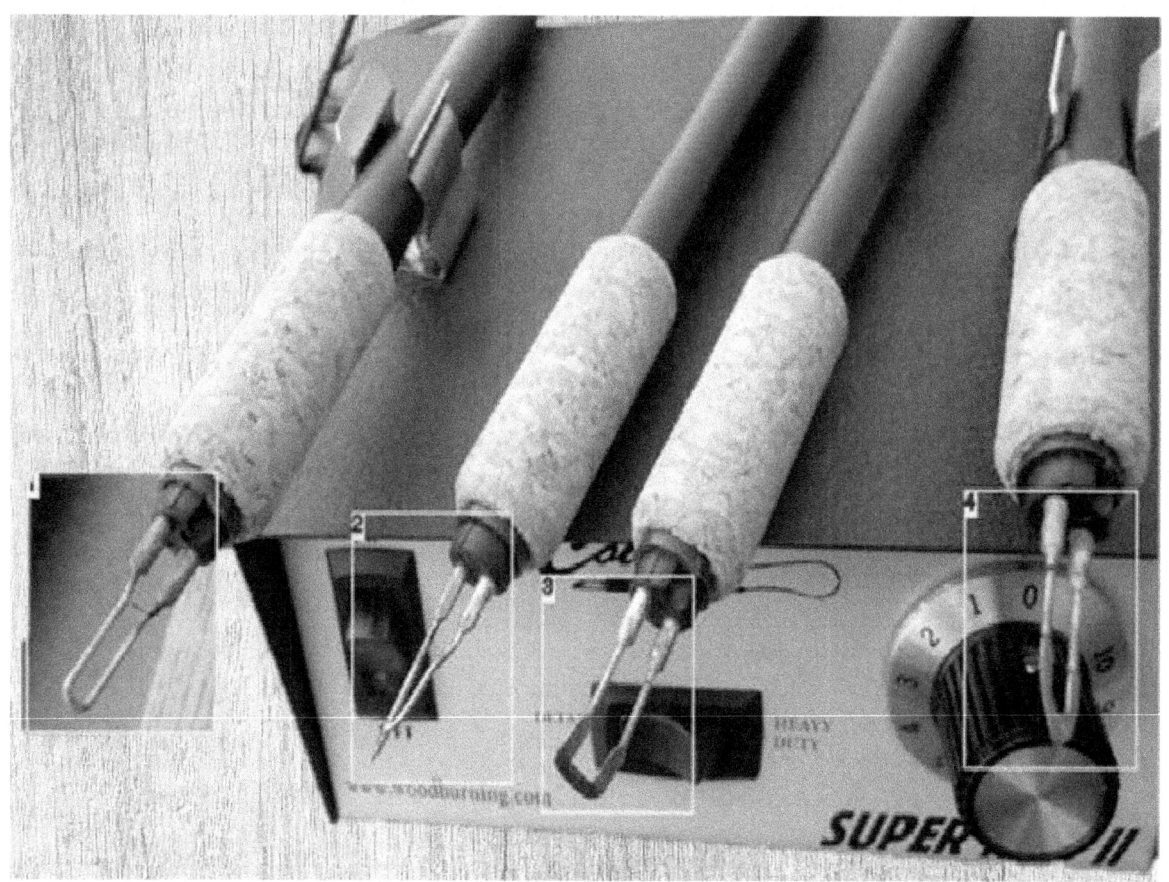

Burner Tip Details

- Calligraphy pen: Used for free handwriting/work and for dark shapes
- Detailing pen: For minute features
- Shading pen: Used for making shiny gradients
- Spear pen: Most widely used! Gives you a very sure and steady tracing

The Setting of Your Hand

No matter the brand or kind of the tip of the pen used for burning, the placement of your hand holding the pen establishes the curves of the lines. It depends on the pressure you put on the burn, and how much time the strokes took.

Your burning pen should be held similarly to your writing pencil or pen. When the burning pen is held appropriately, your hands won't burn out rapidly, as well as the incidence of soreness, and also unreliable burns won't occur. To hold your burning pen the perfect way, your fingers must develop a relaxed grip spread in between the thumb as well as index finger at the tip at an angle of forty-five degrees to the surface of the burning timber.

When you reduce the angle, a thick burn will certainly result, and increasing the angle with the job surface area will certainly give you a thin burn line.

Don't form the habit of permitting your hands to lay on the job been burnt as this does not provide you the liberty to move effortlessly, as well as it influences the length of the burn lines. To achieve equilibrium between your hand holding the pen and also the task, your little finger can rest on the surface of the job and offers the pen tip a company grip to permit you to regulate all aspects of the movement needed for a stress-free burning.

How to Hold a Pyrography Pen

It goes without telling that with a Pyrography job, you'll be investing a lot of time holding your pen. With this at the back of your mind, you must intend to be secure without any type of tension building up over the hours as a result of a poor pen holding practice.

To get going, you require taking into consideration critically the type of pen you make use of when composing with a pencil and a pen. Are you comfortable with a pen with bulk or that which is reasonably light without girth?

When you've figured out this first hurdle, you can, after that, proceed with selecting a machine that has a pen with characteristics appropriate to your hands.

You hold the Pyrography pen in the same fashion that you perform with your drawing pencil or creating a pen. However, a new variable is tossed right into the mix, heat that's generated from the pen throughout the burning process.

Your fingers must go to a range from the burning tip to lower the experience of warmth that would probably be created but not as well much to affect the holding of the pen as well as the work. When buying a Pyrography kit, keep an eye out for pens with safety devices like the finger guard or some type of insulation that minimizes the quantity of heat transferred to your fingers.

The safety barriers give you a stronger hold on the pen. One more tip is to get a first-hand feeling of the pen before purchasing. You can do this by experimenting with a pen your friend has or from an equipment store.

This will help your buying decision. The product itself needs to be reliable equipment that won't be offering you any problem. The pen, which is a vital part of the unit, ought to fit into your hands as well as should **feel like part of your fingers**.

There shouldn't be any doubt of your compatibility with the pen as the relationship would be displayed in your projects. Take your time and explore all offered choices before getting a Pyrography device.

Useful Tips When Working with Your Wood Burner:

A wood burner is a hazardous device. It can cause third-degree melt in your skin as well as can trigger damages to your furnishings or work surface if used thoughtlessly.

Below are some tips to prevent any injury or damage when utilizing your wood burner:
- Buy high-quality needle-nose pliers.
- Some wood burners don't have a button. You have to disconnect them to cool the tip/point used. It would be annoying to await it to cool off before you can change them. The solution is to make use of needle-nose pliers. You can utilize it to remove the tip as well as replace it with another tip.
- Improve your wood burner wire stand. Wood burners include a wire stands where you insert your device when you aren't using it. Nonetheless, you or the people around you can inadvertently tilt it over while servicing your layouts. To avoid this, you can take advantage of this hack:
- Search for an unused/old tile and also glue the wire stand on the tile. Ensure that the tile can cover the tip of the wood burner.
- When you aren't using your wood burner, insert it to the wire stand as well as flip the tile upside down. The wood burner cannot melt the tile as well as considering that the latter is wider, the wood burner would continue to be slanted higher and covered by the tile even if you flip it mistakenly.
- Always put a covering up tape or Artist's tape border when functioning.
- As a newbie, you cannot manage your wood burner well. The tip might slip, especially when

you are dealing with a curved item. Nevertheless, if you have a covering up tape boundary or margin, you'd know your restriction.

- Always clean your wood burner tip with sandpaper before starting a new task. Your wood burner tip will collect carbon as a reaction for heating the wood. This carbon will make your tip plain as well as unequal. You'll wind up with darker lines all the time. To prevent this, always tidy your wood burner tip. In large projects, you may need to cleanse your wood burner tip before you might finish the task.

How to Keep Your Wood Burner Tips Clean:

Cleaning your wood burner can be harmful if you don't perform it right. Below are some tips and actions when cleaning your wood burner tip:

1. Shut off and fully disconnect your wood burner.
2. Let the tip/pointer cool down momentarily.
3. Put on a handwear cover and clean the tip with sandpaper. It's less complicated to clean up while it is connected to your wood burner. Sand it lightly. Keep in mind that you aren't honing it. Your tip will slightly transform in color after time. You don't need to recover its color. Just see to it that there's no resin or deposit of wood that's stuck on your wood burner.
4. Wipe it with soft damp fabric.
5. Dry it entirely before you utilize it once more. Don't let the heat from the wood burner to dry it.

It'll likely produce a reaction as well as will certainly make your lines darker much faster

Using the Wood Burner for the First Time:

Now let's show you how the first attempt with a wood burner looks like, especially for people who can't draw:
When I started with wood burning a few years back and faced an issue initially with handling wood burner, I received advice from the experts about using the burner properly. I share these golden nuggets with you:

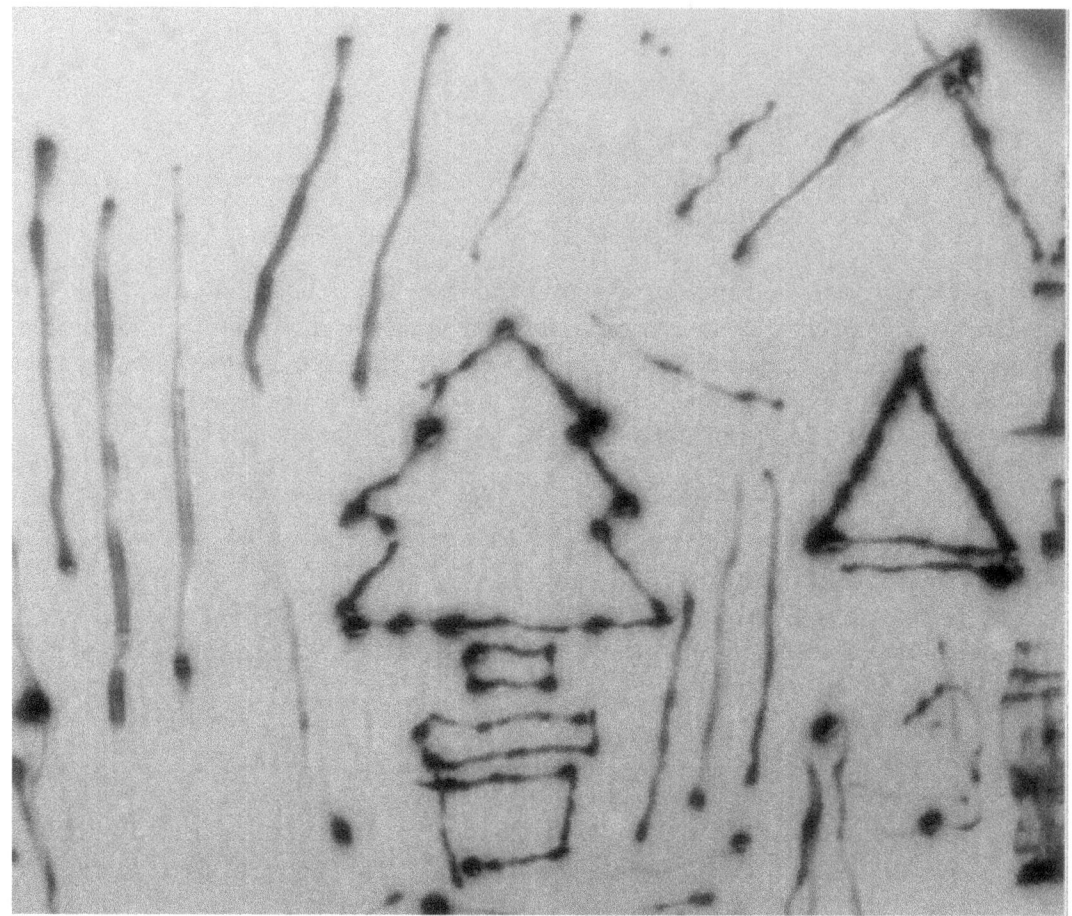

- First, make the wood smooth using sandpaper; this would make things much easier. Also, **do not push** the burner into Wood; instead, **guide it** over the Wood. The guiding should be smooth effort and consistent.
- Sand, sand, sand, and sand some more! Then try a blunter tip if you have medium heat. Don't press down like you are writing. The gentle touch of the tip will make your lines less indented and smooth looking. **Let the tip do the work.**

- Turn your heat down and take your time. You should develop your own rules of how much heat the burner should be for different strokes. Observe and note it down.

- If you can't already draw (like myself), don't freehand burn, draw it up first or transfer an image, or use stencils. Your pyro work would climb up a few notches.

- I think you'll have a much easier time if you practice on basswood or even just sand your wood a bit! Also, it doesn't press down too hard as you go. The tool kind of gets stuck in the grain and causes bumps otherwise!

- The best thing I was ever told was to **act like you're flying a plane - so you're coming into land, and the pen glides in** - it seems to help with the 'blotting' effect!

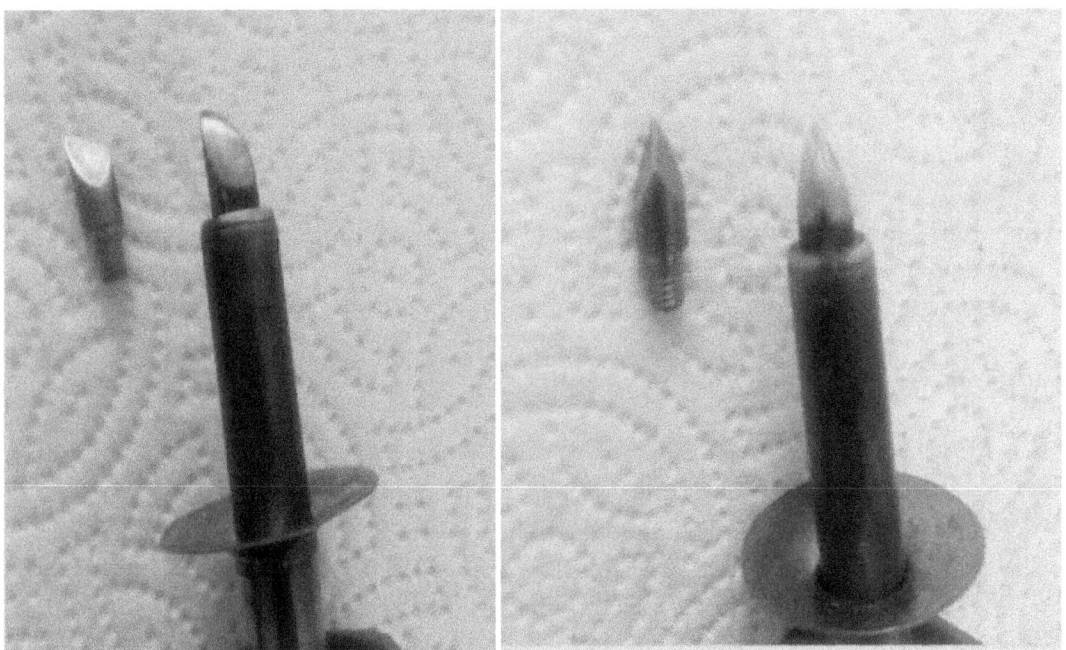

- If you're making use of a strong point, try this. You'll make your cleanest straight lines utilizing a universal tip. To maximize this tip, it needs to be slightly changed. This avoids the heel and also the point "biting" into the Wood. Besides, it's a global tip.

  To make this straightforward adjustment, you'll certainly need a 3M (or comparable brand) of great grit foam sanding pad. Place the flat of the universal tip (while in your heater with it switched off) versus the pad surface area. Apply light stress as well as draw-pull the universal tip back towards you towards your burner pen. Repeat this numerous times on one side. Then button and also make the same point on the level beyond.

  The sponge/foam backing is important, so don't try this with sandpaper alone. The pad will give the heel and toe/tip of the knife-edge a perfect rounding. Everyone who does it is always amazed by the change in performance. You'll achieve smooth, clean lines in no time flat.

- I was told to use this analogy as a guide: think of a plane touching down on a runway rather than a helicopter landing on a pad. Just skim along the surface of the wood with a feather-light touch and yes, sand that wood until its silky smooth. I have a palm sander to work through the grits, since I don't have the strength to hand sand.

- One thing I cannot stress enough is to sand that thing until it's as smooth as a baby's skin! It should feel like silk before you burn, and that will help immensely!

- Try using a lower temperature, and do light strokes, keep hitting the same spot with strokes, so you don't create burn blobs. I initially had that problem, too.

Pyrography tool required along with a Wood Burner

If you're a beginner, you've most likely spent time researching the best wood-burning device to fit your demands. We hope that our resources give you enough r to make your wood-burning projects progress efficiently.

Sandpaper is Crucial for Any Pyrographer

The sandpaper is vital for any item of wood that you're working with actively. You don't want a harsh sensation canvas, and also you do not desire splinters protruding of your artwork! Not only will sanding leave you with a smooth item of timber, yet it'll certainly make wood-burning much easier. Nothing is even worse than running your wood-burning pen along a harsh surface and not being able to obtain the outcomes that you want.

There are electric sanders available, but I've always stuck with doing it manually. I locate that with a power sander, it's simple to take excessive off of the timber as well as leave dips in the surface area. Rather, I attempt by making use of a little block of timber and also wrapping a sheet of sandpaper around it. The grit varieties of a sheet of sandpaper determine just how the surface of it actually is.

Program sandpaper with a low grit number will certainly shave off the wood faster yet will leave a rougher finish. Fine sandpaper with a high grit number will take longer to sand with but will leave it smooth and complete. It's best to start with low grit sandpaper and use higher grit as you go forward. I usually start with 220 grit sandpaper and afterward use 320-grit, 600-grit, and also finally 800-grit. It may appear like overkill, yet if done properly, it'll leave you with an ultra-smooth canvas.

Eliminating Stray Marks

Sandpaper can be used to clear up the stray marks that are caused during pattern transferring or light burning.

Removing Carbon Accumulation

If your Pyrography device is one that utilizes solid tips instead of the cable kind, you'll typically find that cleansing your tips with high grit sandpaper serves often. Check with the user handbook of your wood-burning tool to make certain the best method to clean it before you try this method. Most of the time, I'll keep a small square of high grit sandpaper next to my work area, so that I can wipe any carbon accumulation on the tip.

This carbon buildup as a black location on your tips will certainly take place when burning most woods, particularly something having resin inside. For this sort of cleaning, I generally use very fine grit sandpaper in the 1500-grit range. It'll take away the black areas and will certainly make your tips look brand-new! A clean tip will usually function much better as well as it would heat more equally than a tip with a great deal of carbon on it.

Improving Your Tips

When you're extra experienced, you'll certainly begin to discover what you like and dislike in a wood-burning tool. You can try a bunch of different tips and find that you like having a sharp side on your universal tip. Like I did, you may decide that you wish to make your universal tip a little much less sharp. Few universal tips are too tough to work with if the edge is also sharp as they often tend to cut into the wood. You can take an item of high grit sandpaper and even sand down the side. It is a personal preference that try out and see if it works for you.

Heat Resistant Pyrography Gloves

Many Pyrography artists like to put on gloves while they work. It'll certainly shield your hands if the hot tip touches your fingers and can be a terrific item of safety and security tools. Along with the safety and security facets of using handwear covers a lot of times, they're simply comfier when dealing with particular wood-burning tools. Occasionally some wood burners can be extremely hot and difficult to work with for an extended amount of time. Investing in an excellent pair of gloves will certainly enable you to function longer and also more conveniently. Several practitioners who aren't used to putting on handwear gloves will say that it's an unnatural feeling, yet you can adjust to it rather rapidly. The key to locating the appropriate glove is to pick one that is safe and, at the same time, not overly bulky. Leather handwear covers are a great choice because they supply a great deal of insulation from the heat.

You'll always want to restrict the product that can melt in contact with the burner. Avoid using a disposable latex glove. It won't offer much comfort from the heat, and it may be even less risk-free than putting on no glove in all. Avoid buying a cumbersome glove that's so thick, that you lose the feel for your illustration.

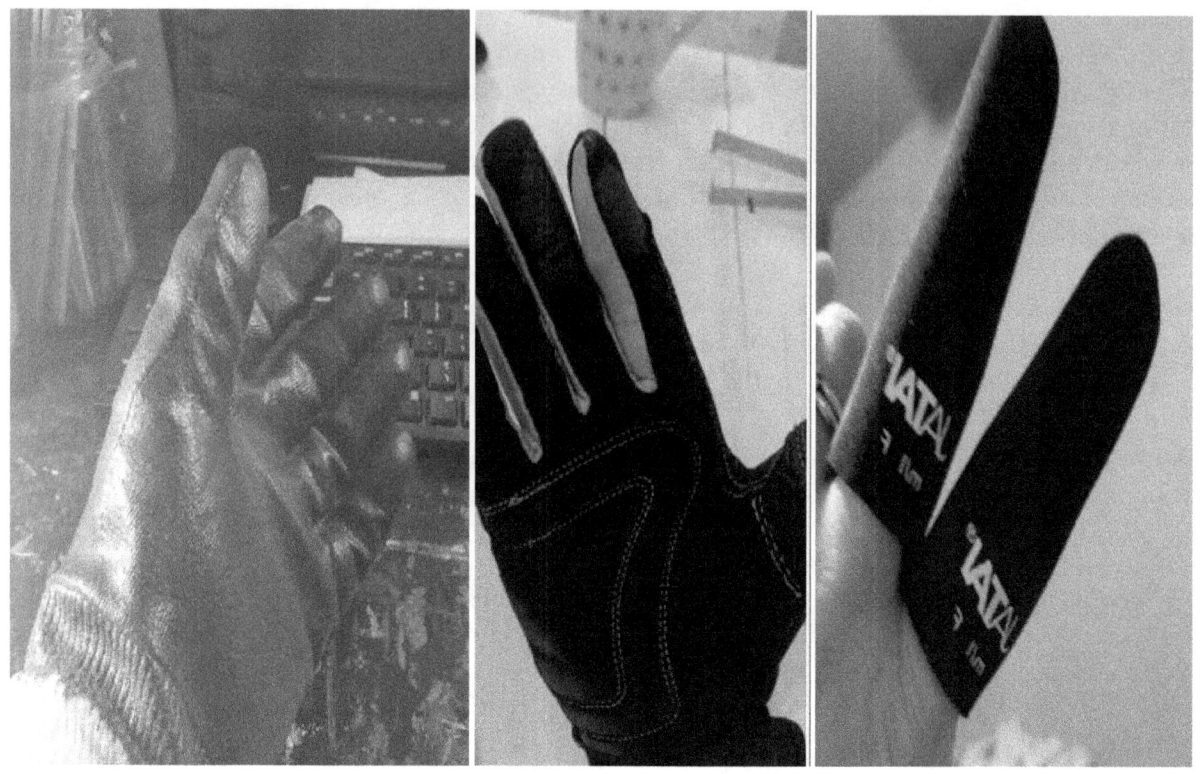

Different types of protecting gloves

Sealer to Prevent Raw Wood Burned Parts from Fading

When you've finished your artwork, you'll want to apply some finish to safeguard your item. One thing that sets apart Pyrography from various other mediums of art is that our jobs change with time. The wood will certainly begin to oxidize and darken over time, and this makes for less comparison between your burned lines and also the canvas. For this reason, it'll certainly show up that your raw wood burning has vanished gradually with time. Unfortunately, there's no other way to quit oxidizing and also fading entirely, but what we can do is attempt to reduce it down with a coating or sealant. In addition to whatever coatings you decide to use, you'll definitely also wish to maintain your complete artwork out of direct sunshine as well as any UV light.

Choosing a Finish

The issue with a lot of coatings is that they make some of your lines disappear or less prominent , and you'll lose several of the detail. We want to avoid this and safeguard your art without modifying it way too much. We suggest evaluating out whatever finishing you choose on a scrap piece of wood to see just how it turns out. Each surface will certainly have various degrees of darkness or color to it as well as some will certainly be extra glossier than others.

Polyurethane

A lot of wood burners like to utilize polyurethane, and also it can be used with either a dust cloth or a brush. Keep in mind that completes like polyurethane will make your raw wood darker. If you choose to layer your art with poly, we suggest satin polyurethane with several coats. They tend to ensure that your surface area is dust-free.

Krylon Spray

There are excellent Krylon spray sealants out there that are easy to use. These can be found in spray cans as well as in many different styles. We use a flat design Krylon sealant to reduce any shine or reflectiveness that shiny surfaces would leave.

Tung Oil

Tung oil can be used on your raw wood burned pieces, yet it'll dim the wood. Tung oil saturates right into the wood and acts to preserve it. It can be applied with a towel and also takes one light coat to do the technique.

Complete for Bark on Raw Wood Burned Parts

If you're making use of a round or plank that has bark on it, you'll want to put a finish on the bark. This will certainly aid to keep the bark in a position to ensure that it does not diminish as well as make a mess. It's typical for some smaller sized items of bark to find off but adding a coating to the bark will certainly help set the external layer and also keep huge items from diminishing. The best tool we have discovered to end up bark is Mod Podge, which can be used with a sponge or brush before or after doing your burning. If you apply it before your wood-burning, be sure that you don't burn any of the bark.

Various Other Raw Wood Burning Devices

Pliers for Altering Woodburner Tips

An excellent set of pliers is a useful device to have for any Pyrography artisan. If you ever find yourself transforming the tips on your iron, you'll wish to purchase a pair. Not only does an excellent set of pliers protect your hand from any heat, it likewise allows you to tighten up the tip a lot more so that they don't come loose. It doesn't truly matter if you opt for a needle nose or typical pliers either will certainly help your demands. I do suggest that you purchase with some type of insulation on the grips to shield on your own from the warmth. Keep away from pliers that have the steel to take care.

Expansion Cord for your Raw Wood Burning Pen

Depending on the device that you have, you may find that you have a short power cord, actually. In some cases, it can be a headache attempting to set up so near an electrical outlet only to find yourself lacking cable. If you have one of the burners that employ a brief power cord, you could intend to consider obtaining an expansion cord. When you're shopping for an expansion cable for your Pyrography iron, make sure that you get one is a big scaled item. These are usually marked sturdy and will be able to better manage the power use of your raw wood heater much more quickly. Some of the smaller sized low-cost extension cables utilize wire that's too small for our requirements. Electrical Safety and security are not someplace that you want to be cutting edges, so don't hesitate to splurge and also to invest a few additional bucks.

Recipe for your Pyrography Tips

One item that lots of people don't think about is some container that's heat resistant, and that'll also hold your Pyrography tips. Although you'll allow your tips to cool down before you eliminate them, they may still be a little cozy and also shouldn't be entrusted to sit on something flammable. Get a tiny glass or ceramic recipe to place your tips in when they aren't being utilized. Not only is it more secure, it's much more arranged and also will save you from tracking them down every time you begin raw wood burning.

Fan for the Fumes

A tiny fan can be a great possession in sucking out all of those nasty fumes when you're working on a piece. It's much more secure to place a little fan to keep every one of that smoke out of your lungs. A little fan can also help to keep the sawdust from your workspace, which can be damaging also when inhaled.

3. Designing, Tracing, and Shading

Basic Techniques

Wood burning is an easy craft. It's practically the like drawing something with burner tip using wood as your canvas. You'll engage in the art of making lines, dotting, and shading. As soon as you get the hang of these methods, you can quickly discover even more development illustrations and also a pattern for your jobs.

Let's see the tips again before starting strokes!

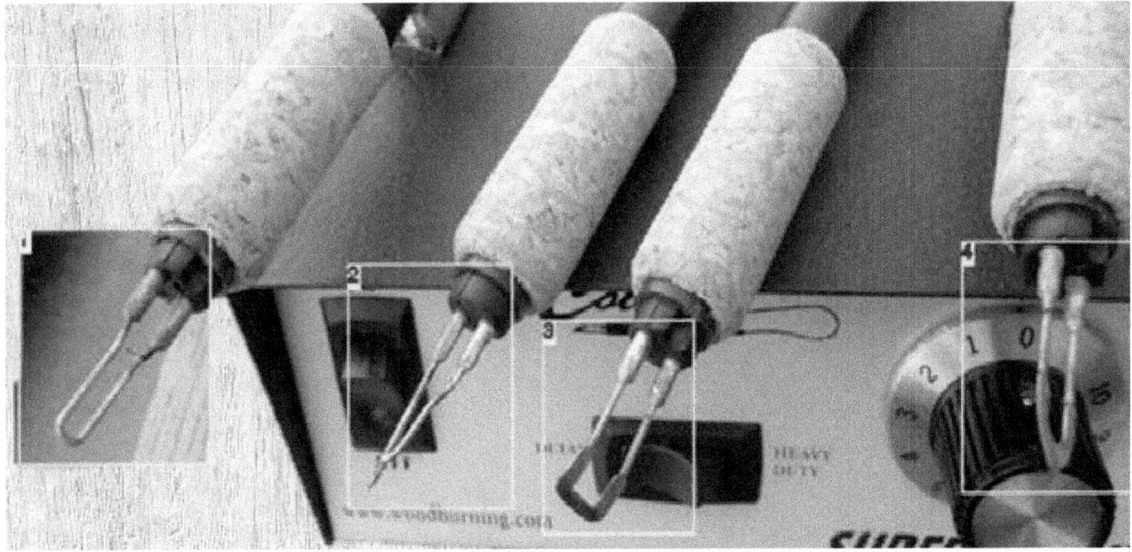

1. Calligraphy pen: Used for free handwriting/work and dark shapes
2. Detailing pen: For minute features
3. Shading pen: Used for making shiny gradients
4. Spear pen: Most commonly used! Gives you a very sure and steady tracing

Practicing Wood Burning Strokes: Get a couple of scraps of wood as well as use them to practice your hand with these basic strokes.

Making straight and also Contour Lines: Straight and curve lines are one of the most typical strokes used by newbie. Straight lines are simple, but curve lines can be a little difficult. Right here is a proven way of just how to manage your wood burner when making lines.

- Place the round point in your side and heat the burner.

- Hold the wood burner like holding a pencil.

- In your regular writing angle, put the point on the wood as well as draw the burner towards you in a smooth way with consistent pressure. If you transform the pressure, the color of your lines could vary. You're beginning with lighter lines if you aren't positive. You can always duplicate the strokes to darken the color or deepen the shade of your lines.

- Always lift the wood burner immediately when you pause or complete doing your strokes. If you keep it on the wood, it'll create a burn a spot, just as a pen would blot.

- When operating in straight lines, make use of a steel ruler as a guide. It'll make things very easy for you.

- When making curve lines, you can utilize two types of techniques. You can map the contour line utilizing the graphite paper and follow it with the wood burner. You can split the curve right into points and link it slowly.

- **Making Dots and Stipples:** Dots and also stipples are used to create complex details. It's easy to do, yet it requires more control. Right here is explained just how to do it. Put a spherical point in your wood burner. Hold it just as you would certainly hold a pencil. However, hold it right above the surface of the wood. Put the tip on the surface as well as let it stays up until you reach your desired dot size. Bear in mind not to press the wood burner on the wood. Let it stay on the surface as well as melt the hole. The longer you allow it to remain, the bigger the dot will certainly be.

- **Shading:** Shading is an important skill set in Pyrography design. It offers dimension and also shades to your wood that a basic varnish can refrain from doing. A wood burner collection often includes a shading tip. It's generally in a spade-shape. Here's how to begin shading your pattern:

Place the shading tip. Don't fret if your wood burner collection has a different shape. Hold the wood burner as you would hold a pencil. Put it in an angle where the entire flattened part of the tip can touch wood. Shift the wood burner in the circular motion to provide the gradient effect. Keep in mind that the longer your device continues to be on the same spot, the darker the shading will be. If you aren't certain or unsure of exactly how dark your shading would certainly be, do it

Progressively shed the area on a lighter layer and also repeat the shading instantly you intend to dim. Unless you wish to make a spade-shaped design, don't press the tip on the wood.

More Advanced Strokes from Various Other Wood Burner Tips: When you fit with your strokes, you can currently try to make use of various points besides the ones recommended. Some other wood-burning points that you can explore making use of after some method include:

The universal tip: It's one of the most important and common tips. It resembles the calligraphy tip; however, it's thinner. Using this tip is easy to navigate like the round point; however, it's challenging to regulate the width and also the depth of your strokes.

You may require practicing it before using it on your jobs. You can make dots, lines, and also shading with the universal tip, yet be mindful. The strokes you might make can be irregular as a result of its level tip.

The Calligraphy tip: Some wood burner features this tip. It's a slim, rectangular, and also flat point that makes bigger strokes. It's typically made for drawing letters and curved patterns with differing thicknesses.

Making Holes in your Wood:

For a project that utilizes thin or tiny woods, you might need to use your wood burner to make holes. Using your wood burner to make the holes may take a while; however, you could require it for some of your jobs.

It's easy to make holes by utilizing your small or large round tip. Simply hold your wood burner as you would while making dots. Allow the tip remains on the exact same spot for a very long time. Press only lightly and also allow the wood burner to do the remaining job. For a cleaner surface, after you have actually burned a hole via the front, flip your board and also put the tip from the back. This is also to make the hole on both sides.

Designing

There are several methods to create the design on your wood with wood burners. You can do it straight if you're positive about your skills. However, mapping the design to the wood is suggested for novices as well as for those who aren't positive in their illustration skills.

There are two prominent ways of moving your patterns to your product. You can either trace it by hand or make use of a tracing/transferring device that you can make use of from your wood burner seller. Below is a conversation to explain exactly how to do both means.

Mapping/Tracing Technique:

The usual way of tracing your pattern on your wood is by mapping it over the graphite paper.

Below is how you can do it:

Print or draw your pattern on a clean white paper. Be sure to make matches of your original, so you can quickly replicate it when you make a mistake while mapping it. Put the paper over the wood and slide a graphite paper in between them.

Make sure that the graphite side is on the wood. Trace your pattern on the wood utilizing a pencil or a pen. Press securely to guarantee that the graphite is moved to the wood, along with your design. When done, eliminate your layout and the graphite paper. Darken the lines with a pencil if they are too light. Don't over darken the lines as it may end up being difficult to remove. Utilize your wood burner to map the design permanently into the wood.

Utilizing the grey part of the gray-and-white eraser, eliminate the graphite and pencil lines from your design. You can leave your pattern as it is, or you can tint or use finishing on your wood.

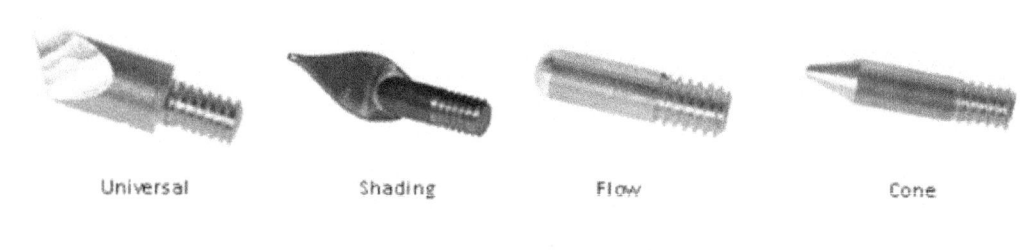

Walnut Hollow Burner Tip Examples

Flexible Mapping/Tracing

Mapping in rounded areas of your project with simply the paper as well as the pen can be challenging. Experts usually utilize thin non-fusible interfacing to map their patterns on rounded areas. You can purchase the interfacing in stitching stores.

Don't make use of the laminated or fusible ones because they'll certainly leave visible lines that are difficult to eliminate. Right here are the steps on just how to transfer on a contour area or wood. You can draw your design directly to the wood/leather. Nonetheless, it's advised that you publish your pattern on a notepad and also trace it on the interfacing with a pencil or pen. Slide a graphite paper listed below the interfacing.

Ensure that the graphite side would certainly face the wood. Making use of masking tape, connect your design to the curve location. Affix them with the boundary. This isn't essential; however, it'll help you deal with the layout on the wood as you trace. Trace the design by making use of a pencil or a pen. You might need to push more because the interfacing is thicker than a routine paper.

Gradually peel your layout as well as trace your design by adhering to the guidelines.

Photo Transferring

An additional way of mapping a layout to your wood is my photo transfer. It's faster as well as smoother, yet you require certain tools for it. For this procedure, you'll definitely need a printer and the tracing tip.

The Tracing Tip

Not all wood burners feature a mapping tip; however, some let you buy it as an extra accessory. It's usually a flat huge round tip, and it is much heavier than most of the tip. It imitates an iron, yet you can use it to make large dark dots for your styles.

Exactly How to Transfer the Photo to the Wood

Print your wanted design or picture in notepad using a LaserJet printer. The ink-jet printer would certainly not function well on the wood. Place the paper in addition to your wood. The picture must be facing down. Fix the paper making use of a covering up tape if you need to. Affix the tracing tip on your wood burner. Put it on top of the paper and iron the back of the paper in a circular motion. Make sure to cover the whole paper. Repeat the process twice to make certain that the layout is transferred well. Be careful not to go beyond the paper, or your wood will certainly have burnt parts. Slowly eliminate the paper. Darken the lines that are too light with a pencil. Trace your layout by adhering to the actions of the standard mapping strategy.

TIP: If you're moving a big photo on your wood, you can utilize your iron as opposed to the tracing tip. You need to be careful, though. Iron can burn your wood and the paper .

Mapping with a DIY Stencil

There's another technique on just how to transfer your style to your wood. It involves utilizing a Do It Yourself stencil and also chalk. It's a cleaner technique but has restricted applications. You can only do this for styles with solid as well as constant styles. Nevertheless, this technique is excellent if you want to replicate your layout or duplicate your job.

Below is exactly how to achieve it:

Materials:

Paper cutter, double-sided paper, tape plastic, binder separator, translucent as well as colored chalk

Directions: Publish your wanted pattern on the paper. Once again, this is just perfect for solid styles such as letters as well as straightforward mandala patterns. Place the binder separator on top of the paper. Inspect your layout and mark the places you must not reduce for your stencil. If you have a part in the center that would diminish if entirely cut, mark it with a tinted pen. Cut your desired pattern. Bear in mind not to cut some parts of your significant areas. As soon as your stencil is done, position it over your wood. Shield the cutout rooms with the colored chalk. Eliminate your stencil and burn the locations with chalk.

Note: Be careful not to remove the chalk traces with your hands. Clean with a towel to eliminate the excess chalk.

Including Shades to Your Layouts

Your styles will have a far better dimension if you add colors. However, it can be difficult if you utilize normal wood paints, especially if you're a novice. So, as beginners, include color by utilizing wax pencils, gel paints, as well as wood stains. These materials can quickly be removed and appropriate for a newbie.

Using Wax Based Oil Pencils or Crayons: Wax works better with the wood. You can apply them with your bare hands as well as manage the deepness of their colors. You can remove them, making use of the gray-and-white eraser if you make a mistake. You can sand off the shades gently if you want to lighten them. If you wish to blend the colors, you can utilize your fingers or cotton bud to do it.

Using Gel Repaints: Gel paints may not be as simple as the wax-based oil pencils. They stay in the area longer than normal paints. There's a greater danger than you may mistakenly smear them. Nevertheless, this trait of gel paints makes them great material to tint your wood. You have a longer time to do different brush strokes or make special results on your designs. If you make a mistake, you can clean the paint from the wood. The issue occurs when you require the inclusion of one more shade. The shades might blend and generate a different color than the original. Yet, don't stress. The solution is straightforward, before adding color in addition to another shade, make use of a soft clean towel to take in the excess gel paints. This technique will dry the paint faster and will allow you to include a new layer of colors to the wood.

Using Wood Gel Stains: Gel stains work like fluid stains, but not as dripping as the last. The wood doesn't absorb them excessively. Thus, the grains of the wood will still show. The genuine wood look of your artwork would be maintained. Gel stains are additionally available in different colors, which you can easily blend through a paintbrush.

Making Strokes with a Wood Burner

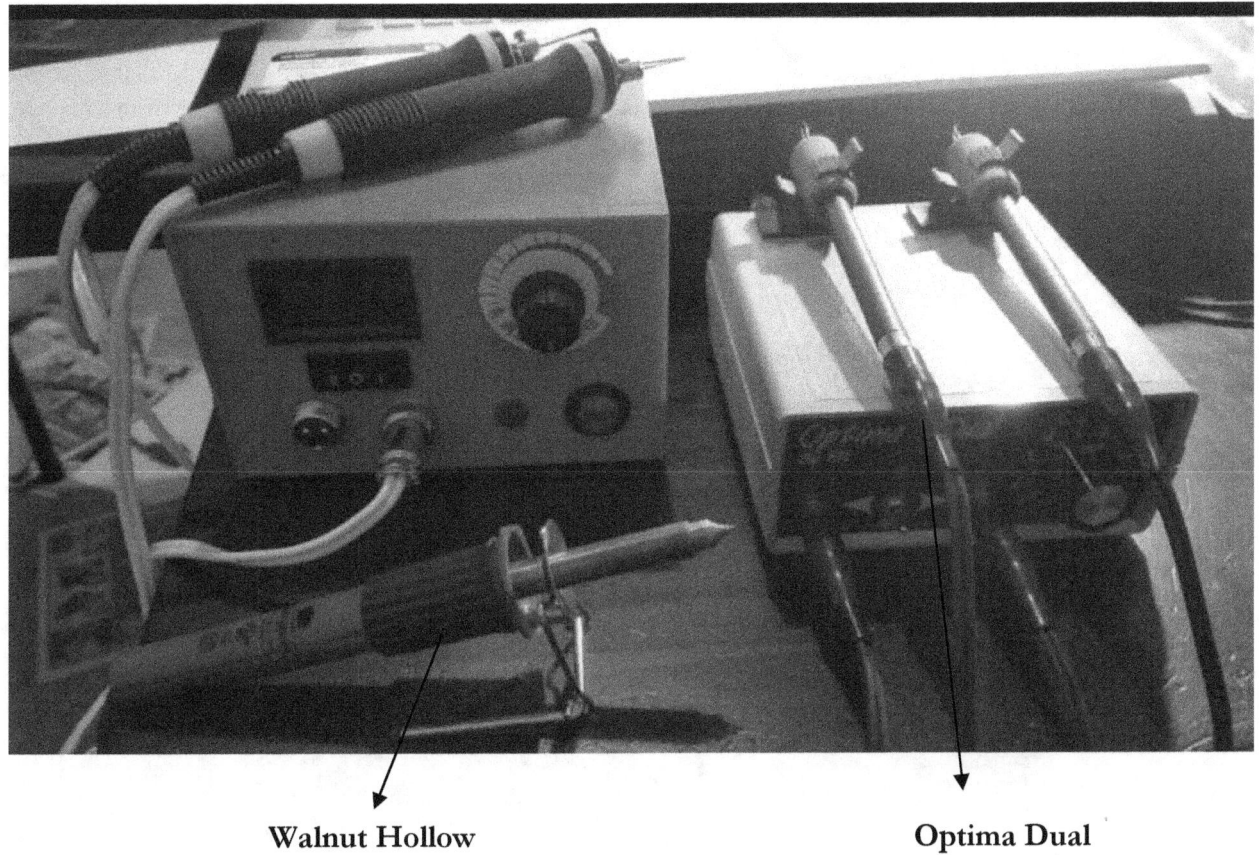

Walnut Hollow   **Optima Dual**

Fundamental Strokes with Wood Burner

Before you can do your wood-burning, you require the tools that go with it. One of the most standard wood burners we make use of is **Walnut Hollow**. (Generally referred name in the Pyrography community)

They're called such as they're the manufacturers, and also, they include a control, so if you're able to acquire this, you'll see there are controls from low to medium to high.

- The first thing, of course, is to always bear in mind the fact that it gets very hot. This one shown above has rubber on it to avoid your fingers from obtaining as well warm.

- And also never leave it warm on its own because someone might touch the tip as well as burn them.

Now we additionally work with this great even more remarkable tool from **Optima or Razertip** (Again, as far as a company name, you can get a similar product from other companies as well).

These are slightly pricey, yet they work wonders when doing wood burning.

Now before you can do wood burning, you have to learn some basic line methods which you can attempt while working on a piece of wood.

We used birch originally.

So let's start!

While initiating this art, the first things you find out are the fundamental line techniques, and also, these are the lines that you begin with, the line between 2 points. Straight lines are the shortest distances.

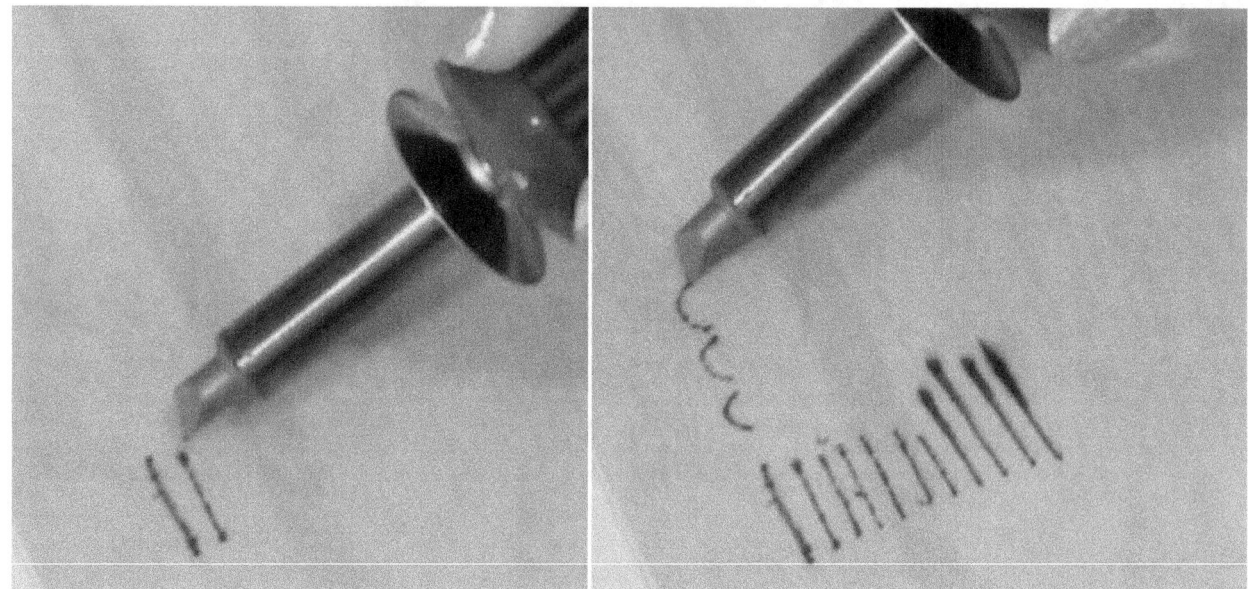

Straight Lines Curves using edges

Once you're holding this wood burning tool, it's excellent to find out initially how to regulate by doing a few of those straight lines. If making use of just the point, we're going this way, yet if you make use of the entire edge of the tool, you'll get this. Relying on the stress of your hand, you obtain a darker line.

Now when I'm going stronger on it, and we're doing a burning of the wood right there, and you can see the power of fire. After you do some straight lines, you can start doing some curved lines.

Going in the direction of the right using just the pointer and doing it rapidly, you can see the type of lines that you're obtaining.

Currently, I'll try to do it going in the other direction as well as see if we can achieve a far better contour. Considering that I'm a right-handed person, so I don't generally yield a good one out of that. However, if we again do the whole side of the device, you can see it's almost like doing calligraphy where you attain a slim as well as a broad line.

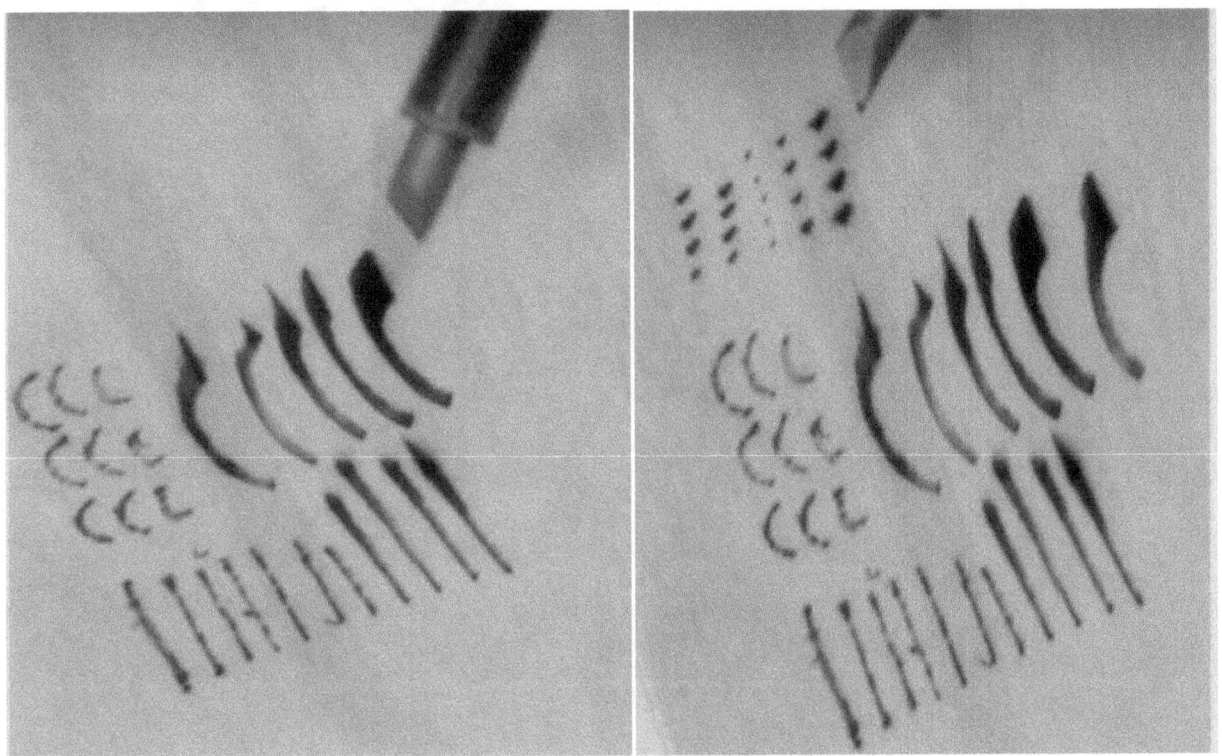

Curve lines like calligraphy **Light, Medium and Heavy pressure points**

If you've ever before tried calligraphy, you can see these sorts of lines appearing of your pens. And also, wood burning is similar to pen and ink job, except of course you're making use of electrical power you are using the power of fire.

After that, there are times you can do these kinds of lines like stippling or simply populated lines. If you do light pressure, you get small little dots. With medium pressure, those are the kinds of lines you obtain. After that, you're digging deeper, and this is how you improve control of your wood-burning device as well as practicing in this manner will make your skill better. So then you can do meandering sort of lines like just squiggles when you scribble. Now, this device is thick, so we won't get a very easy effect on this set.

However, little wood-burning bits can be made in several sizes, so relying on the thickness or the heaviness of your tool, your styles will vary, and I'll certainly see a lot more about that in a while.

When we do waves once again with this, as you can see, there are some limitations to this kind because it's thick. However, there are truly great little bits that you can utilize, and also you'll be surprised at the type of lines you'll eventually draw from them.

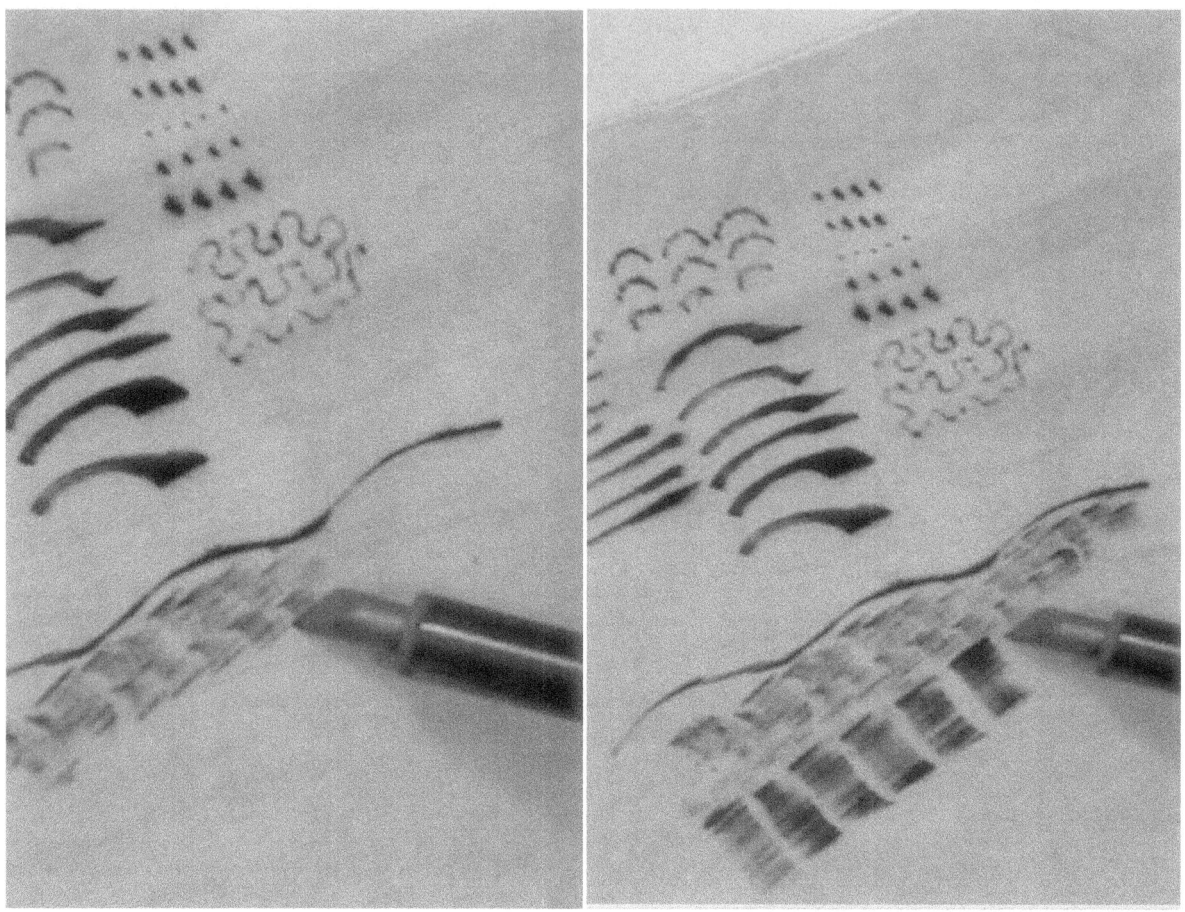

Meander, Waves and Shading   **Dark Shading**

Right here is now something you can do with this heavy device. This certain one is shading. It's nice for shading. Mild touches are the trick to obtain great shading without burning your job. So there's a different type you can try. Feel the thickness that you place on your wood. In some cases, it's much like a touch, like a little stroke, and also you'll get extremely nice and also gentle shading.

And then you can go deep as well as hefty on this and also you can see the distinction. And remember this tool is just one of the heaviest wood-burning bits that we have.

You'll be impressed with what the finer tools can do. So now, I want to transform this device right into a finer one. You switch off your controls, and then you switch off the wire to this wood-burning device.

It's better to be safe than sorry, and at the same time, after you do that, be careful because the tip is still warm, and we can make use of a pair of pliers to reverse that.

Now this brand-new little bit, which is slightly smaller or half the dimension of the initial one that I collaborated with, so it's hot enough so we can use it.

New Finer Tip   **Sharper Straight Lines**

Our straight line is simpler to start with as well as the device is easier to handle, and also, the lines you get are much cleaner and also finer. Plus, if you like a straight line, it'll truly do a straight line for you.

Everything relies on you; you remain in control. Don't let the wood-burning tool control. You're always in control.

And I'm using the entire side of it. If there's a little resistance from the wood that you'll certainly feel as you're working on it, and that straight line is challenging to achieve.

Yet if you use the entire side of it and it works as smooth, similar to butter. Now we can attempt doing rounded lines with it once again. Once more, this is much more cooperative than the various other devices because the tip is thinner as well as finer.

We're doing some zigzags currently. So these are some standard line methods that you might intend to do. When you learn more about wood-burning, it's like simply playing. You won't find it tough whatsoever; it's a lot of fun to do as well as it's similar to doodling.

If you like scribbling, you can utilize your pen or your pencil, but this moment you go one degree higher, you make use of the wood-burning device.

We can do some meandering lines once again, many like little zigzags or curves that enter any kind of direction as well as you can likewise do squiggles or spirals.

Shading is additionally possible from dark to light, but you don't obtain large protection immediately. It's unlike the larger tool that we attempted the first time.

So currently, you can see the distinction between the sizes as compared to the very first device that we attempted. And a combination of all these fundamental line strategies creates any project with various shades and lines in it.

Suppose you wish to make a circle like that. For the most part, when we do a circle, it's simply a flat circle, but if you wish to color it, you shade it as well as it starts to make the circle into a sphere because you place the third dimension to it.

The first step is to do a circle, and after that, you put some shielding because you act there's light being available from the tip side, and also, the left side is dark because there's no resource of light and also it becomes a sphere.

The darkest component will get on this component on the left side, where there's no resource of light. And also naturally underneath that will undoubtedly be the shadow produced by your ball. So it remains on the table right away where it rests is the darkest. And after that, you do a little shielding on this component as well as you enjoy. You can make it right into a basketball, or it can also be an apple. So an apple is most likely nicer to look at.

So, this ends the introduction and tip on using wood-burning devices. I suggest you buy any of the burning tools shown above first.

| Trying different shading | Drawing Circle |

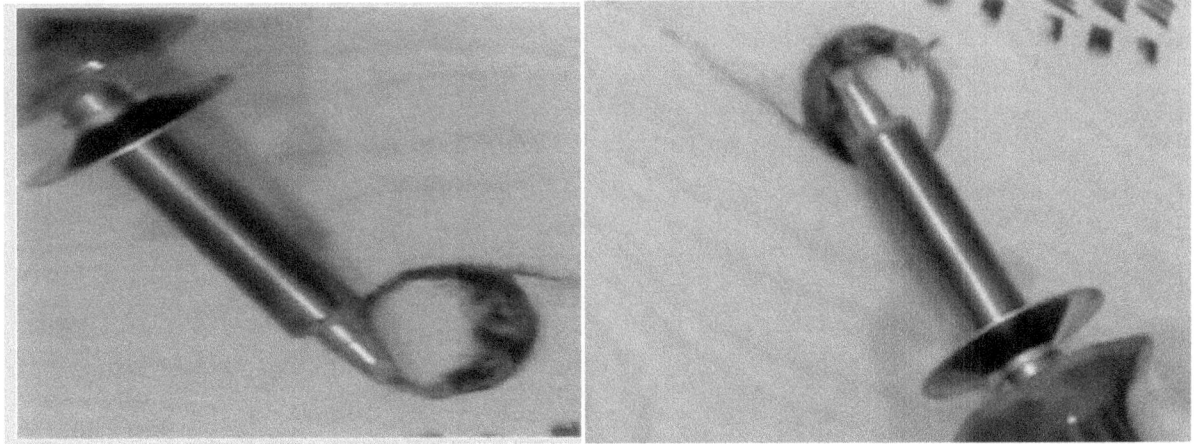

| Shading the Ball | Make it an Apple |

Pyrography Shading: Tonal Values Boxes

Let us discuss the tonal values and how to use heat for more shading.

Let's start with the very lightest shade and work our means up to the darkest shade, making use of several different shading techniques and heating levels.

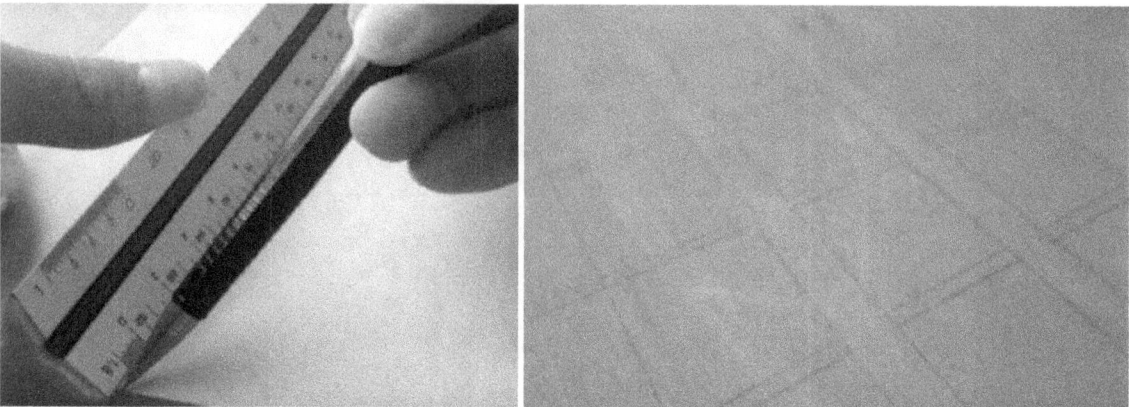

So let's now begin by quickly drawing out a number of these tonal value boxes this way, we can obtain them side-by-side and also compare our forms.

- The First technique is **round movement**. Start with a low setting of 3 with a sharper tip. Also, utilize a very straightforward round motion by making small little circles. Repeat this process until you obtain the required tone.

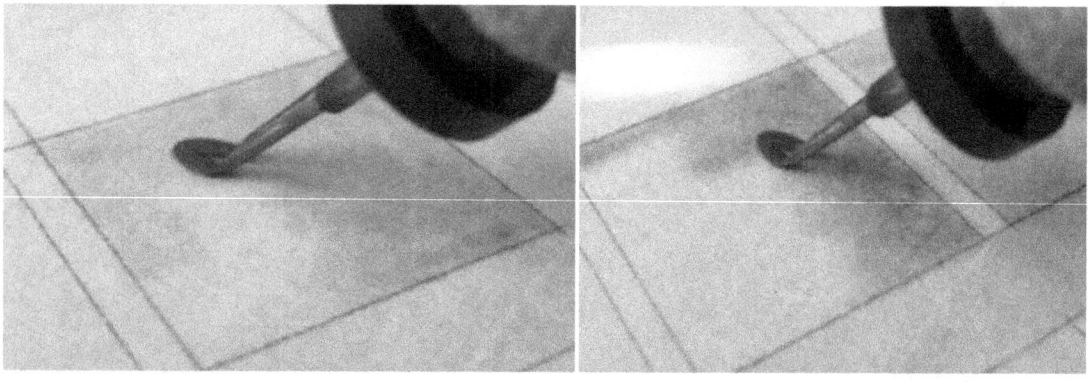

Heat Setting 3.5   **Heat Setting 4**

We'll maintain the heat setting quite low if you wish to burn actually light as well as I'll go much faster if I wish to keep it lighter; however, if you keep your heat setting low, there's no requirement to stress much regarding burning too dark. We'll turn the heat up to 3.5, and also we're going to get a little darker.

It's my preferred shading technique by using that round pattern; the shader doesn't remain on the wood too long, and it doesn't create a hot spot in one area as well.

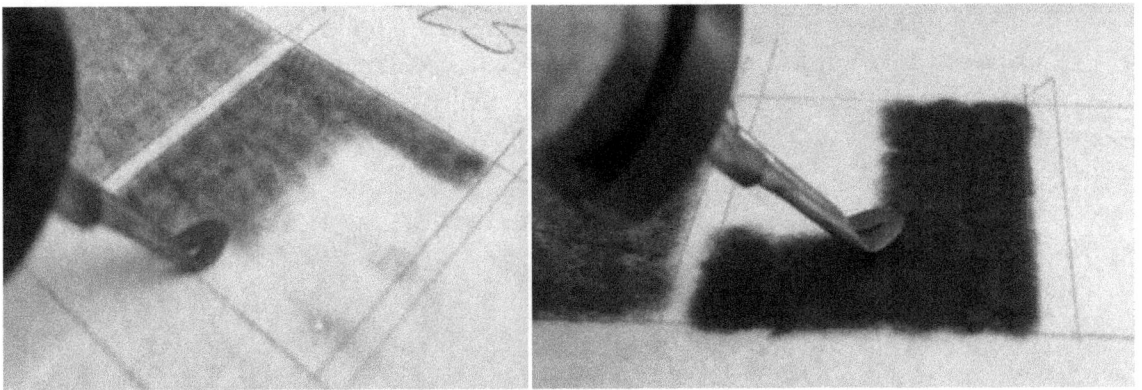

Heat Setting 5   **Heat Setting 7**

I have the most control over the circular pattern than any other technique that I utilize for each tonal value. Now we'll turn the heat up a bit to make sure that we can keep the very same pace, and also, we're going to proceed with this circular movement throughout and maintain exercising obtaining the next tone.

- The next shade is the very technical term, the **pulling movement**. This is where you simply pull your shader tip across the surface of the wood and do utilize this technique occasionally. It's not something we utilize a lot since we have found that it's not hard to do; it's just that it's really simple to develop a darker spot in a location when you don't want to.

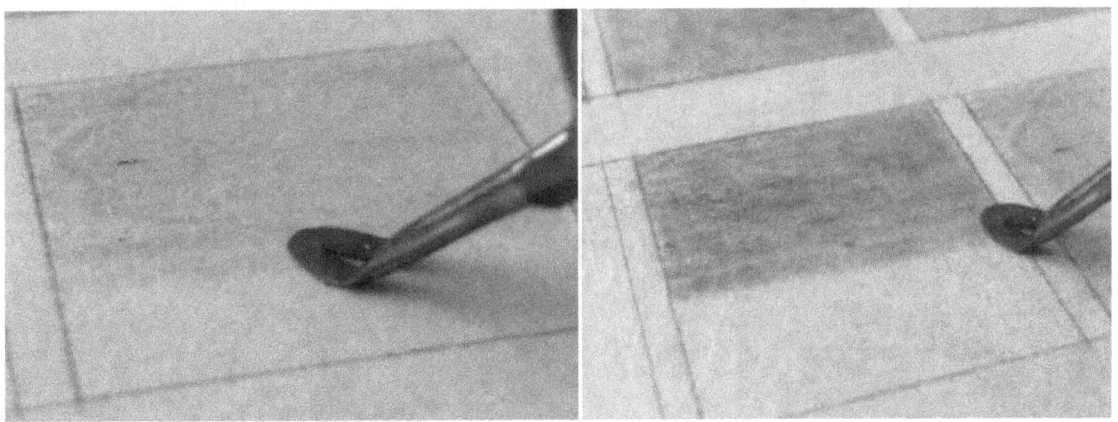

Heat Setting 3   **Heat Setting 4**

So let's transition to the following shade we're going to increase to 4 right here, and also you can see it's a little bit darker than our previous shade and we're simply going to continue this motion on and just pull the shader tip throughout the surface area of the wood and also try to obtain the wanted shade.

We're going to up to the heat setup of 5 to burn a bit darker. That also means dark when I get my sanding pad as well as send this out genuinely fast. So currently, we've got it back to the tone that we desire. I'm still on heat setting five here yet if I hold my shader on the wood a bit much longer. It'll give us a bit of a darker shade below once more. I'm at approximately six, and if I go a little bit slower like depicted below, you can see it's much darker.

Heat Setting 5   **Heat Setting 6**

- So right here's our last strategy: the **dot pattern!** As you can see, this is simply a basic dot pattern. I've got my round tip right here instead of the shader tip, and you go through your shading locations with a dot pattern you set your heat, and also, you leave your burning tip on the wood according to exactly how light or dark you want your tone.

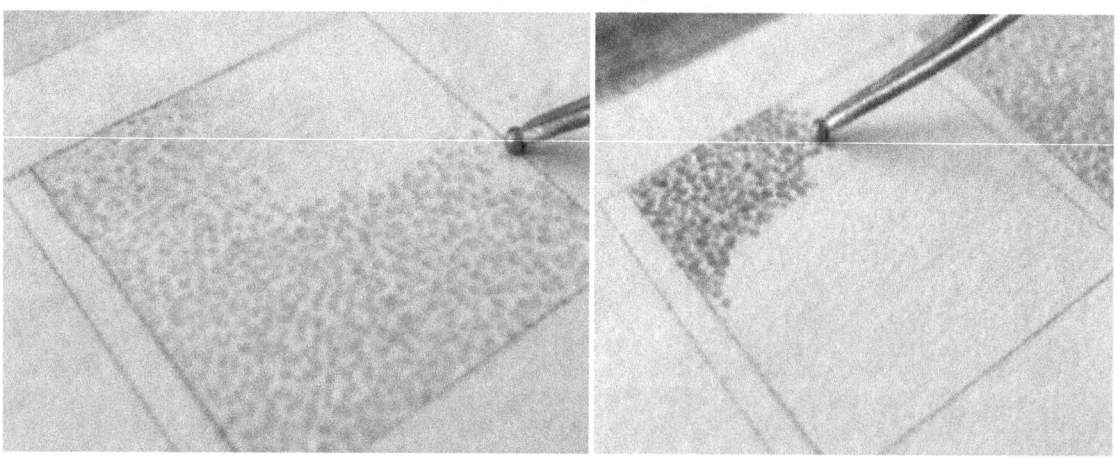

Heat Setting 3   **Heat Setting 4**

We're going to increase the heat a bit right here. Let's get a little of a darker pattern. This is what I see a lot of wood burners use. It's not something I use a lot even as I don't have the persistence to do all the little dots. It's, however, very effective for a shading strategy, and also, when you're finished with this kind of pattern, and you're done with your entire item, it gives a very amazing appearance. Although it does take longer, it does give you more control over your shade.

Heat Setting 5   **Heat Setting 6**

In the end, I'm right up on six as well, as you can see exactly how deep it's going into the wood. It's simple, so we've tried all seven tonal values using each shading strategy you can see in the photos above. Again, each shading strategy provides a bit of a different texture and has its worth, and also it's very own quality. Lastly, you just need to find out which is the best burner for your job.

Several Tips and Tricks for Shading

Over the years, I've provided and received many advice and tips based on burning experience. I'm now sharing a few of those for your benefit from that discussion with my co-burners!

Below are the Tips and Tricks on:

- **Drawing and Transferring Pattern/Picture:** On my initial projects, I put a lot of effort into drawing by free-hand. I felt I'd be cheating if I did any transfer to the wood. Ends up, I was wasting time. As I started to get more orders with great deals of various motifs, I realized people do not care about it. What truly matters is the burning itself, since that's the final result.

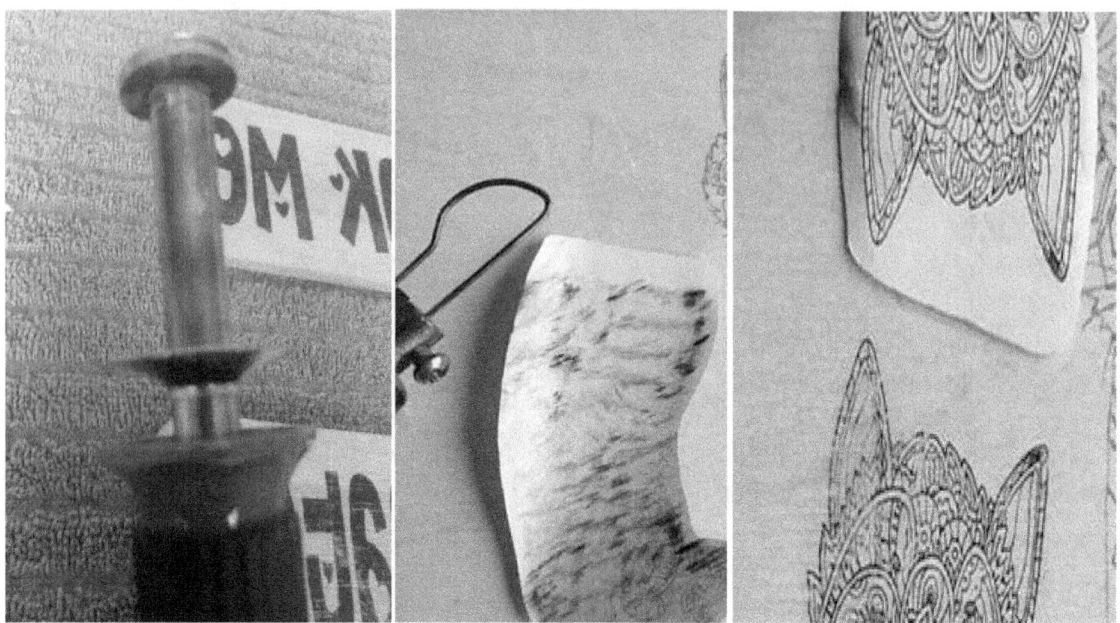

Image Transfer Tip **Image Transfer Example**

So currently, I use black carbon paper/graphite paper (using blue is a disaster, trust me) to make the transfer, and some free-hand. Indeed, from time to time, it's still great to do an entire project in the old design.

Trick: Some individuals print the illustrations and also transfer the toner from paper to timber with heat, making use of a usual iron or even a heat press. Make sure your picture looks precisely how you want it to be in the wood, given that you'll certainly not have control over which lines will be moved. I choose to have finer control over my edge lines. Also, it can warp the timber if you're not cautious!

- **Filling shapes**: Filling in black is continuously much easier than making slopes and can be equally as beautiful.

For large surface areas, I recommend a flat gradient tip in medium to high heat (see fig1). For small spaces, the calligraphy pen is genuinely excellent (see fig 2).

Trick: Don't try to fill your illustration using as much heat as possible, unless you wish to leave ugly stroke marks all over. Work with medium heat with soft circular movements, and also slowly darken each area at a time.

Golden method: Delicately blow on your tip as you touch wood for the very first time, as well as let it heat naturally as you move in a short round pattern. It'll ensure a smooth start! The warmer you apply, the extra dark your outcome will undoubtedly be. Apply this tip to produce contrasts versus shiny gradients.

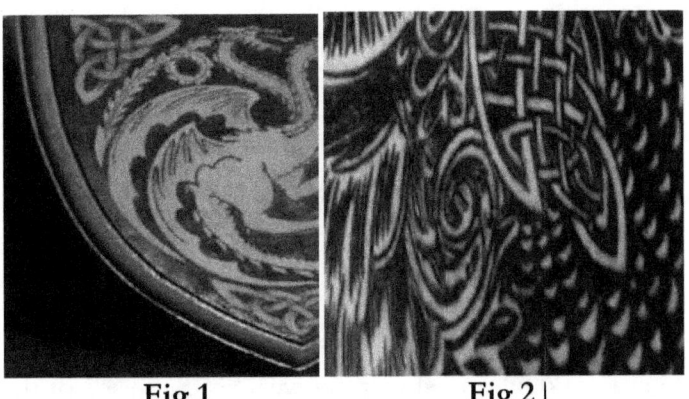

Fig 1   Fig 2

- **Gradient impact**

Making Gradients is more complicated than filling black because you require much less heat, even more patience, and also finer control.

We always utilize a flat tip for this work and also instead use a wood burner with temperature level choice. For the majority of timbers, a 4 to 5/10 temperature degree is what you require.

Practicing Gradient   **Expert level gradient**

In this instance, start gradually with circular movements as well as warm-up one little area at a time. In the beginning, you won't discover any adjustment, yet slowly the shielding will undoubtedly turn up. It's always less complicated to move along surrounding areas because they're currently warm than move back and forth amongst remote regions of the surface area.

Trick: Beware with the timber grains, since you won't have the ability to burn as effectively in these areas. If you have large grains, they'll undoubtedly make gradients much tougher to craft/burn. You can always attempt to use more heat in these areas.

- **Hatching**

    Hatching and also cross-hatching can offer you a stylish effect of shading and even appearance without the difficulty of making gradients. They may also function better when your wood is rough.

    For this method, make use of a tracing tip (like the spear-shaped one) as if you were sketching any other line. Start by hatching in one direction, always beginning by the sides; by doing this, the stroke will certainly burn stronger in outline, and slowly get weak in the inside of the illustration.

    To make your shading genuinely stand out, attempt some cross-hatching by including an additional set of lines vertical to the very first.

Hatching   **Cross Hatching**

- **Textures**

    There are unlimited textures you can mimic by burning, so I've to give some methods for a few additional ones:

Hair: For insane hairs, which are merely a little messy, utilize the flat shading tip with a higher temperature level. This time you don't require to be smooth because you want to leave direction marks around. By controlling the stress, you can range dark black strokes and also softer shades. To make it less complicated, you can begin by outlining the hair quantity as well as delimiting blank spaces for the lighting.

Hair and Beard Example

Fur: A tracing tip, either sharp or rounded, can produce an excellent effect of brief as well as soft hair and make up the shading. The principle is to use more temperature as well as closer strokes in locations you want to look darker, along with less and also faster strokes where you intend to be lighter. If you assume the total appearance is too sharp, smooth your lines with a level shading tip.

Fur Examples

Scales or leathery skin: Time to make use of sharp and broken lines, to produce the impact of the braking surface. Use a flat tip for shading, causing the sides truly dark to create volume. Don't use hatching in this situation, unless you want to end up with a hairy dragon.

- **Background Technique**

    When you're done with your burning, it's time to think of the background. It can make a terrific difference in the total appearances of your task, particularly when utilizing a cheap-looking item of wood.

    The following methods are suitable for all levels of wood-burning projects:

    Rust: Without a doubt, the most convenient method, when you don't have anything to lose. I utilized to take a couple of rusted screws and also bolts, and also remove a few of the rust with sandpaper. To use this on the wood, spread dust in the surface area with chalk or charcoal. If you do not wish to obtain reddish fingers, use a cotton ball instead.

    At all times, I used this method. It's fascinating to make your background opaque when the first burning has a glossy gradient, for it'll truly stand out.

    Heat blower: A heat blower can be made use for a terrific vignette impact. Turn on the blower as well as move along the edges. Never blow at the very same spot for greater than a second. Move along the whole area and heat it uniformly. It'll take a while for you to begin seeing some shading, but once it starts, the process is rather exponential. Be extra cautious with the metal tip of the warm blower so that it won't touch wood or your skin.

    Shading or filling up:

    If you hold your horses enough or you don't have large locations to fill up, you can attempt some gradient loading or even take a complete black method. In some cases, the full black background is a demand for art, yet this is honestly a horrible lot of work. My tips would certainly be: just do it if you're certain that the final result will be worth it, or else the background will give you more difficulty than the actual job.

    Dotting:

    It's a very old strategy, as well as can be discovered in some medieval art items; already, it was done by heating metal bolts and "branding" the wood multiple times with them. Currently, even the cheapest wood burner will certainly come with a big round tip for this kind of work. Wait till the burner is really hot and fill up one dot at once. Also, clean the tip whenever it accumulates way too much carbon.

Sample Background

4. Coloring, Polishing, and Finishing

Finishing

In Pyrography, finishing can make or break your artwork. After getting done with the wood burning, the item looks much better when you apply some finishing. Thus, you need to recognize the standard on exactly how to make your artwork stand out without ruining your layouts.

Standard Finishing Method for Pyrography

There are four basic ways of finishing your woodwork. You might require these strategies to provide your Pyrography project with a tidy look.

- **Wiping**: Utilize a tidy, soft, and also completely dry cloth to clean the dirt, erase powders, or any residue from your finished work. Experts suggest that you always have to wipe your work each time you finish a design or eliminate the traces. If the dust is hard to wipe with the use of a dry cloth, you can utilize a wet fabric to clean your finished woodwork. Yet, see to it that you wring the cloth well, so no water leaks from it.

- **Sanding:** Some parts of your wood would certainly be rough after you have burned it. You cannot simply clean them off. To cleanse those rough spots, use fine sandpaper to smooth them. To do this, cut only a tiny item of the sandpaper. Thoroughly as well as lightly, scrub it over the part you intend to finish. Some portion of the sandpaper might touch your actual style and also damage it if you utilize a large piece.

Coloring examples

- **Applying mineral or olive oil:** A shiny woodwork gives it a robust beauty. Applying lacquer and also various other varnish materials can offer your artwork a nice sparkle. However, it can be tricky, especially if you used tinting materials in your wood. Expert developers apply mineral or olive oil rather than lacquers. It'll certainly provide your wood the shimmering result without mixing any shade to the wood. The oils will enhance your wood as well as maintain the color intact for a long time.

- **Using lacquers and shellac:** Applying layers of lacquers, as well as shellac, can lighten the burned color of the wood. If you desire a genuine wood look for your artwork, using these finishing products can be the trick. Professionals suggest darkening the burned styles if you intend to use them. Shellac and also lacquers additionally toughen the wood, making your artwork last longer. The best way to apply them on your finished Pyrography project would be through spray-on, particularly if you made use of colored pencils as well as gel paints. Utilizing the brush would certainly smear the shades.

Utilizing Finished Wood as the Base

Plain wood isn't the only product you can use for woodworking. You can likewise add Pyrography designs on painted and finished woodworks. A colored history can provide a nice touch to your wood-burned task. It can be complicated and also a bit harmful, mainly if any ignitable product is used for finishing of wood.

Thus, when including or making use of finishing materials to your Pyrography job, you should think about these tips:

- **Usage water-based tint:** Some designers finish their base wood with water-based tints. You can do this by weakening dyes on the water and also apply it on the wood using cotton rounds or soft towel. The dye would certainly tint the wood, but will not cover the grains. It is risk-free, non-flammable as well as does not emit fumes when burned. However, it takes a while before you can make use of the wood for your task. The wood would soak up the water, and it would certainly be hard to burn your style over it. You require drying out the wood for 2 to 3 days before you can utilize it for your job.

- **Usage water-diluted glaze:** Another safer product to finish your wood before starting your Pyrography is the acrylic polish. You can make this by weakening the acrylic paint on water. The portion of water and paint varies relying on how thick you desire your polish would certainly be. Include even more paint if you desire your glaze to cover a lot of the grains. The glaze will omit fumes when you burn your designs. However, you don't need to dry your wood for a very long time. The thinner polish will result if you include much more water than paint. It'll work like a water-based color. Hence, you might require drying the wood for a couple of days before you can begin with your project.

- When utilizing an oil-based finishing product, position your woodwork in an open as well as a ventilated room: Oil-based finished woods will create fumes when burned. It can asphyxiate you if you're operating in a closed area. Additionally, oil-based materials are inflammable. It may develop a fire when burned. You can conveniently control the fire as well as decrease the damages if you're working in an open area.

- Watch out for the carbon deposit in your wood burner. Burning a finished wood makes your tips keep carbon faster. Therefore, you always need to cleanse your tips after a few minutes of burning.

** It would be even better if you avoid using any finished/human-made wood for the project because of possible health issues. Follow the next chapter on safety and health before any other instructions!

Various Finishing Oils

5. Safety and Health Concerns

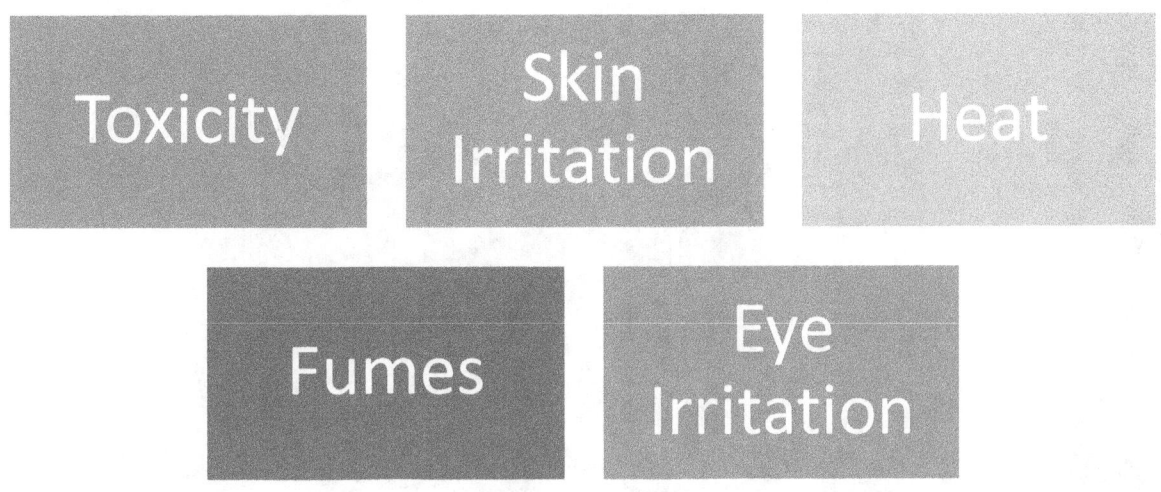

Pyrography can be a really enjoyable leisure activity; however, there are numerous risks/dangers involved that you need to know. We get asked a great deal concerning the security of the craft, particularly when it comes to inhaling fumes created while burning timber. While this is an obvious problem, there are other things you must be aware of before you enter wood burning. Along with the fumes, there's an actual fire threat, along with dangerous sawdust that could act as an irritant to your skin.

Smoke Inhaled

There are a lot of variables that impact how unsafe this smoke can be, so it is best to be on the safer side. You ought to do your research as well as ask a professional regarding the toxicity of each timber type that you select for burning.

All the fumes are more or less harmful to health if inhaled. Therefore, proper safety measures should be taken with the first aid kit in place.

Even if there's no chance to alleviate the threats completely, you should do your best to minimize them.

I keep some fans blowing and also a home window open up to ensure that the location I'm operating is well ventilated.

It keeps the smoke out of the area and also out of my lungs. Choose woods with fairly low poisoning levels. Since there are a lot of alternatives readily available to us, there's no reason to use woods that produce harmful fumes.

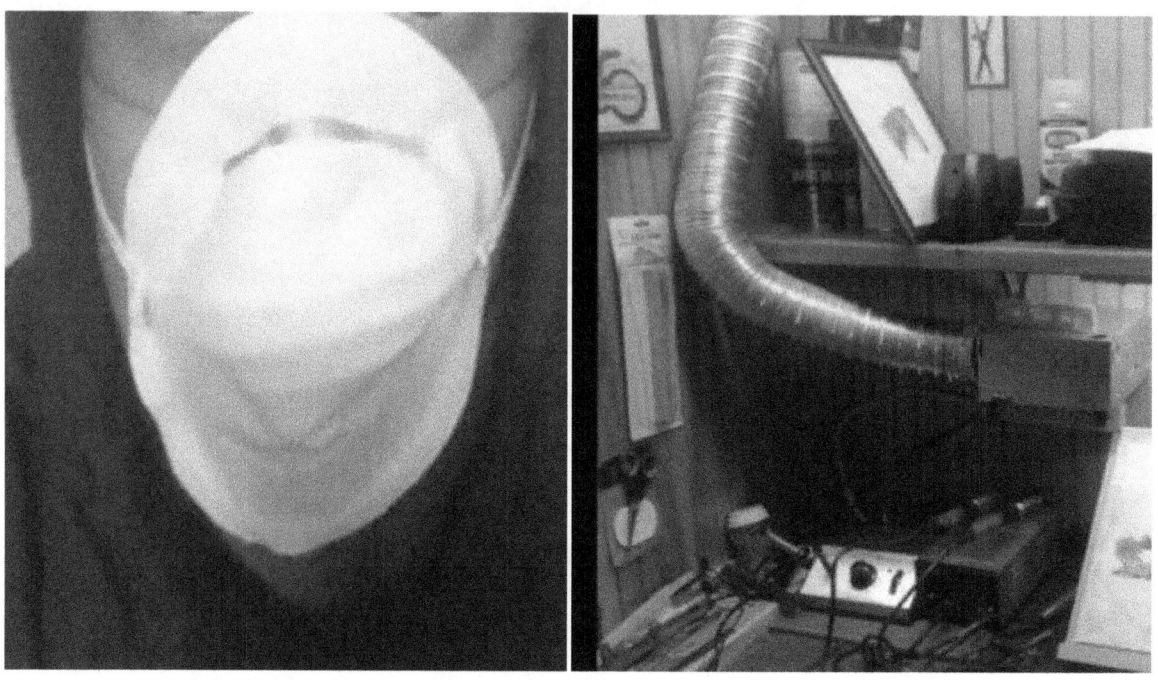

Sample Mask   **Smoke Exhaust**

Woods to Avoid

It's also crucial to stay clear of utilizing any wood that has been repainted, stained, stress treated, built, etc. Also, after hefty cleaning or sanding, the chemicals from these procedures can still be deep in the timber, and even burning them can be very damaging to your health and wellness. As a general policy, **stay clear of dealing with any wood that is manufactured or man-made.** Synthetic woods consist of MDF (medium-density fireboard) and also plywood. MDF includes formaldehyde, which isn't something we wish to be collaborating within Pyrography.

While some artisans choose to deal with plywood, it can be hazardous to your health if you burn through the timber layer and also start thawing the adhesive. Because of this, we avoid it entirely.

It's worth it to acquire some excellent fresh-cut wood and also avoid this undesirable carcinogen. In case you're residing in the countryside, you could be able to get your very own fresh timber that is free from any human-made chemicals. You must consider consulting your local lumber lawn to see if they'll deal with you to give some great cuts.

We have had success acquiring good canvases from scrap timber at several of these lumber backyards. Instead of getting rid of these leftover pieces of scrap, they volunteered to assist us in filling it as well as they even cut it up perfectly, so that we could use it.

Just go, smile, and ask for extra wood, and it could work as it worked for me most of the time! While it isn't constantly that simple, you can typically buy scrap or remaining wood from these sorts of areas for rather inexpensive.

Wood Identification

You must recognize what species of timber you are burning and research it before you start. (There is a ton of information about toxicity level of fumes from different woods also available online).

Each timber has distinct attributes as well as toxicity degrees. You may be influenced by the smoke from one type of timber, yet not from another. Along with your health and wellness, we ask you to take into consideration those around you also. Consider any person that may enter your workplace and may be exposed to the smoke or sawdust. Your wellness and also the health of others isn't something to ignore, so please do your research study before starting.

Sawdust Exposure throughout Pyrography

While the smoke is the very first concern that enters your mind, you should likewise know about the sawdust produced. The dirt developed when sanding wood is also a risk of being inhaled into your mouth, nose, throat, as well as lungs. It might likewise be an irritant to your skin, along with the sap launched in your canvas.

The primary step is to sand outside your working area. This keeps the dirt away from your workspace. Some artists pick to wear gloves when dealing with timber as certain kinds might be an irritant to your skin. Once more, this is something that you need to seek advice from a professional before choosing a variety of timber to work. Only an expert will certainly have the ability to give you accurate updates on all of the health hazards of a particular species.

If You Observe Health Problems, Stop Working Immediately

If you're burning and you discover difficulty breathing, have any burning sensation on your skin, eyes, or throat, or establish a rash, you must call your doctor quickly. It's possible that the fumes, dust, or sap have resulted in these irritations.

I don't want to scare you, but prevention is always better; nonetheless, I feel that you should know the risks. I directly have never had a problem when timber burning, yet that isn't the case with every person. I aim to educate you about every little thing feasible, which includes safety and security problems. There's no harm in using a mask when sanding or cutting timber to be on the risk-free side.

Precautions from a Hot Wood Burner

It still requires highlighting to some brand-new beginners that your wood-burning device will be hot. You ought to recognize its temperature level and also placement at all times. I don't suggest leaving your timber burning tool for any length of time while it's connected.

While these are excellent tools, they're capable of beginning fires and injuring youngsters or grownups who may not know them. Always work responsibly and also bear in mind the state of your devices. Make sure that the cable of your device does not offer a tripping risk. This may injure another person or pull your hot iron off of its stand and also onto the table or flooring. Even if you understand your hot timber burning device, you ought to anticipate to be burned if you deal with it long enough.

Many times I've absentmindedly allowed the hot end of my timber burning tool to touch my hand or arm. Let me inform you it is not an enjoyable experience! Some artisans wear gloves to avoid burns like these as well as to shield their hands from the heat. Relying on the heat setting, your hand may end up being fairly warm after a long session! Different timber burning devices may supply much better insulation than others. Some come furnished with a guard of kinds that will obstruct a few of the heat up as well as others won't have this feature.

Speak With a Professional!

We aren't specialists on the subject of safety and security, and we don't declare to be. We wish to enlighten you on several of the risks included, but at the end of the day, each person is responsible for one's very own safety and security. We hope that you do your research study on wood that you collaborate with, which might include talking with an expert. It's a great tip to ask about harmful effects that might result from burning, handling, cutting down, or sanding the particular varieties of wood.

6. Starter Projects in Pyrography

Now let us see how we can apply all the knowledge and create some small projects to begin. So get excited and review the real-time application of whatever we've learned until now.

1. Wooden Dominoes Game

Wooden Block used for Domino

Materials needed:
- 30 pieces of 1" by 1-1/2" timber
- Little as well as huge round tip
- Sandpapers with fine grain
- Cotton balls Mineral or olive oil (optional).
- Colored gel paints (optional).
- Ruler and pencil.
- Gray-and-white-eraser.

Direction:
- Sand each wooden item. You can acquire a long plank of birch wood as well as demand the

craftsperson to suffice in the sizes you require. You may also buy it from specialized crafts shops.

- Using your ruler as well as pencil, divide the leading surface area of the timber into four equivalent parts.
- Place the tiny round pointer on your wood burner and wait until it warms up.
- Using the pencil guide, burn the straight line on each item. Repeat up until you reach your preferred shade. Utilizing the picture above, draw or trace the outlines on the wood items.
- Use the tiny round tip to draw squares that need three or even more dots. Use the large round tip to draw the "1" and "2" squares. Dim the dots if you don't want to include any color.

Wooden Dominoes Box

- If you prefer to include color, gently sand the surface area of your timber and also wipe it tidy. Using the gel paints and a tiny tip, Chinese brush, color the dots, and let it completely dry entirely.
- Dip a cotton sphere in a percentage of olive or mineral oil. Wring the cotton extensively to remove the excess oil. Brush the oil on each of the domino cards.
- After a day or more, clean the domino and also use it.

2. Key Holders

Keyholders and coasters are my favorite projects for beginners. The key holders come in many shapes (square, circular, and triangle). They're super easy to draw and a great gift for holidays. You can also drill and make a hole in it for the key.

Materials Required:
- Keyholder rings
- Spoon Point Nib
- Craft Knife
- Spear Nib
- Bladed Nib
- Eraser
- Pyrography Unit
- Pencil
- Blank wooden key holders

Sample Key Holders

Directions
- Either draw the image on one side of the key holder, or you can get the printout and transfer it from the graphite paper and carbon paper. You can use a pencil or image transfer nib. This method is the easiest way and takes little time to transfer on many key holders.
- After copying the image, at medium temperature, use a bladed nib and burn the lines.
- Keep turning the key holder while burning the drawing to avoid pain in your hand caused by maintaining one posture of the hand for too long.
- Using a spoon nib, shade the image, and letterings on the item. You can introduce an element of gradient shading or whatever other forms of shading you want.
- Replace the nib with spear point nib set to a high temperature. Then proceed to burn a fancy pattern around the edge of the key holder. Choose beautiful designs that will appeal to those you're going to gift, sell, or exhibit.

3. Wooden Jigsaw Puzzles

Materials Required:

- 2 item 8" by 8" birch timber
- 1/2 inch thick published design template of a cartoon character or any other design
- Gel paints Mineral oil shading tip little and large round tips

Examples of Wooden Jigsaw Puzzle made using Pyrography

Instructions:
- Sand the surface of the timber.
- Using the printed layout, trace the character on one of the wood planks making use of the pencil and the graphite paper.
- Draw an overview of the personality/design using the round tips.
- If you have a laser burning pen, you can utilize it instead.
- Darken the lines somewhat.
- Change to the shading point.
- Apply some color outside the traced picture/design.
- Aim to make the image draw attention after you use the shades.
- Color your picture using gel paints.
- Dry your timber for at the very least 2 hours.
- Flip the board inverted.
- Making use of a pencil, split the wood into any number of blocks.
- Following the lines as the guide, draw some wavy lines over the straight lines. Use these curved lines as an overview to cut the board
- Sand the sides of each puzzle chip to give it a smooth coating. Apply olive oil on the sides, if preferred.

- Keep and assemble the chips on top of the ordinary birch timber to reconnect your drawings.

To prevent damaging your drawing when cutting the puzzle chips, bring your finished artwork to the equipment store. They have tools to cut wood right into preferred shapes. They'll help you out for a small fee.

4. Wooden Alphabet and Numbers

Materials Required:
- 7 pieces 2x2 wooden dices or 28 pieces (if 1 for each alphabet)
- Wax pencils or gel paints
- Olive oil
- Calligraphy tip or universal tip
- Small round tip

- Laser prints of the alphabet and also number 0 to 9. Include another collection of vowels and another piece of zero.
- If you prepare to tint your blocks, use prints that'll certainly permit you to trace the summary of the letters. If you aren't using any, use font styles that are necessarily 1" in size—sprayer or cotton buds.

Instructions:

- Sand the timber cubes. You can acquire these cubes at crafts stores.
- Using your pencil as well as ruler, draw a verge on each face of the cubes.
- Burn the borders making use of the little round tip.
- Utilizing your laser print outs, transfer or trace the letters on the timber.
- Mark 4 letters (a minimum of 3 consonants as well as 1 vowel) and also 2 numbers. Make sure not to put a similar number/consonants on each side of the cube. You can do this by block.
- Using a calligraphy tip, follow the letters using the wide side of the tip if you desire a rustic search your block. If you want your blocks to be tinted, trace the synopsis of the characters making use of the tiny round tip. Sand off the block lightly before including the color of your option.
- Put some olive oil in a sprayer and use it on the blocks.
- Wipe the blocks with a soft cloth or cotton buds. Avoid this if you are making use of wax pencils.
- Dry for a minimum of a day before playing.

Other examples of letters and numbers burnt on wood

5. Coasters

Materials Required:
- Walnut Hollow Versa Burner/Pen
- Wax pencils or gel paints
- Olive oil
- Flat Tip for Image Transfer
- Circular Wooden Blocks

Instructions:

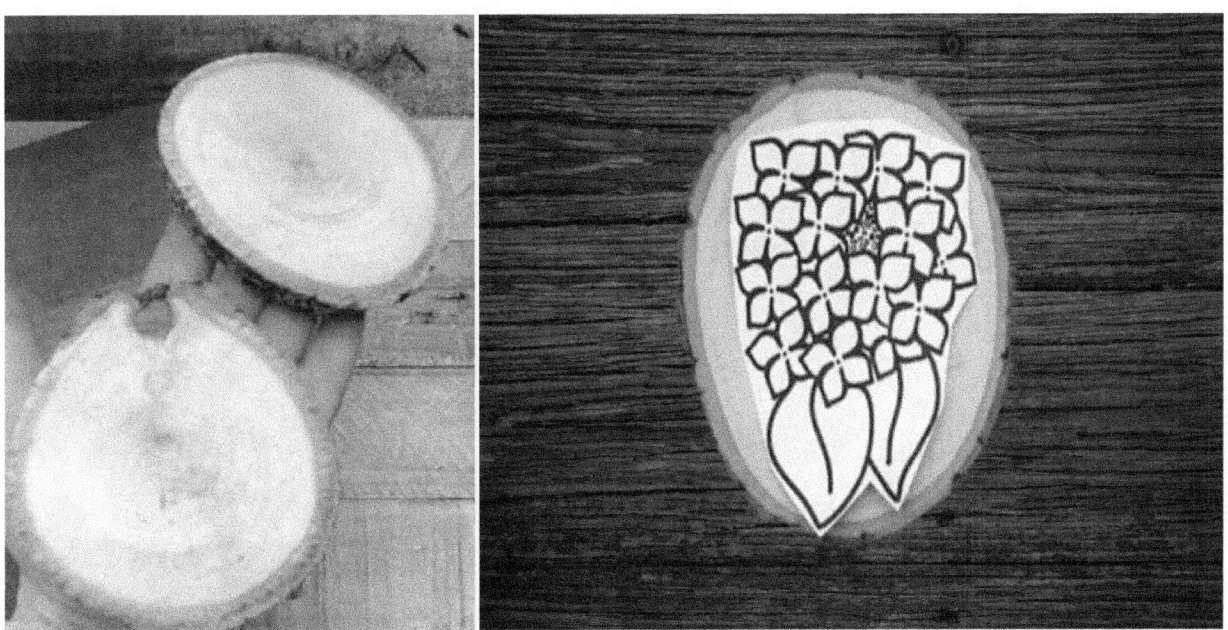

Wooden Blocks   **Design Taken From a Laser Printer**

- Sand the timber piece. You can acquire these circular blocks at crafts stores.
- Draw the pattern/drawing on your I-pad/Laptop and take the printout from the laser printer.
- Put the design printout face down on the piece of wood and start transferring the image using a wood burner, as shown in the diagram below.
- Change the Tip and start running the pen on the image transferred on the wood.

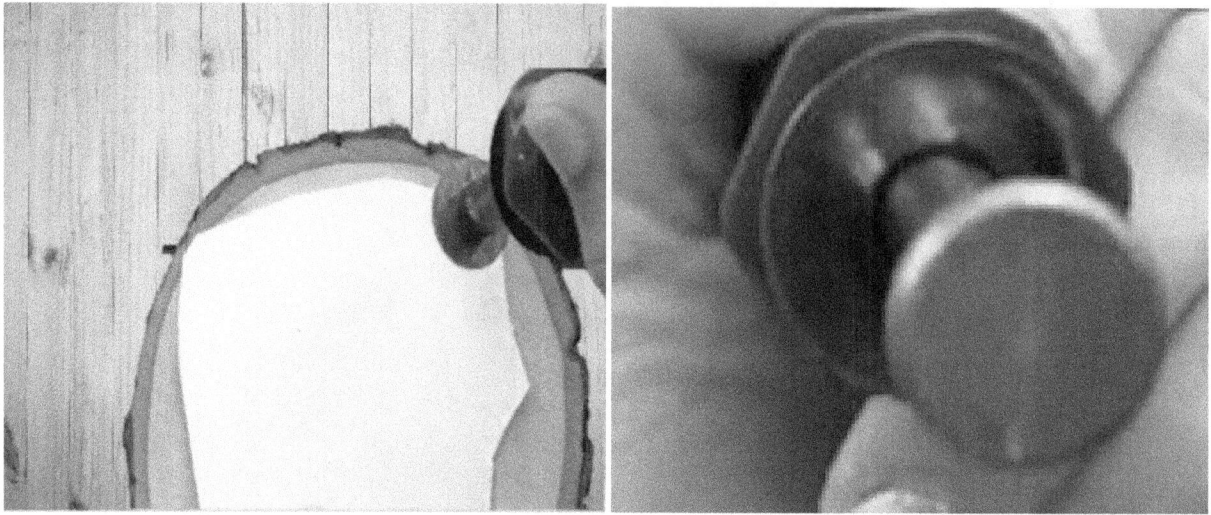

| Transferring the image | Imagetransfer tip |

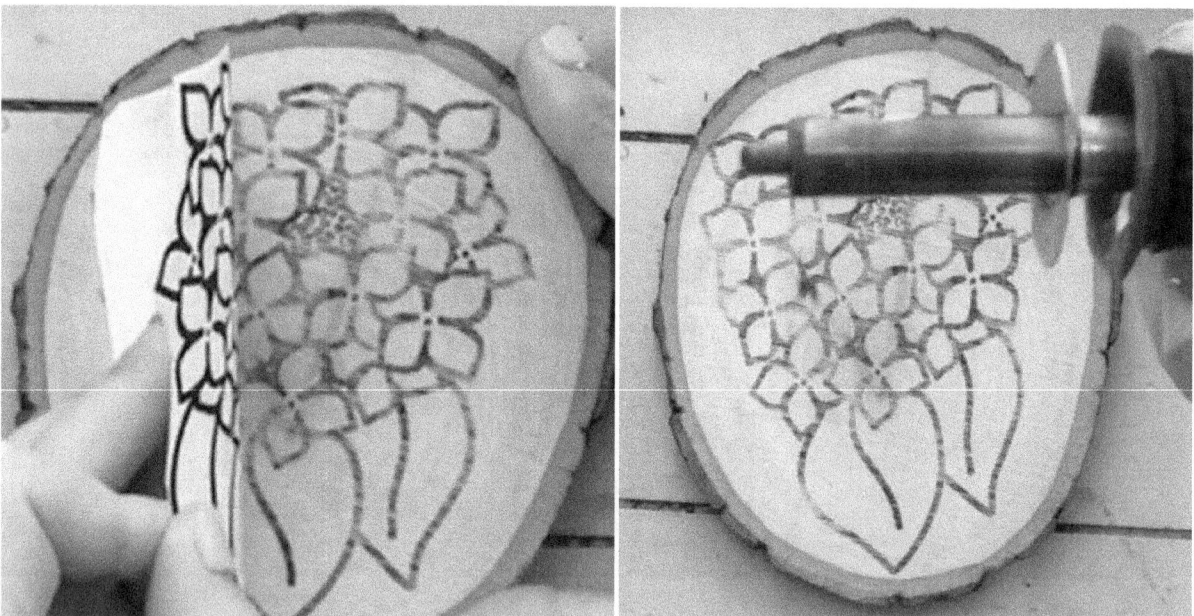

| Picture Transferred on the woodblock | Change the Tip for starting burning |

- After completing the wood-burning along the transferred image edges, start coloring with watercolor, as shown below.

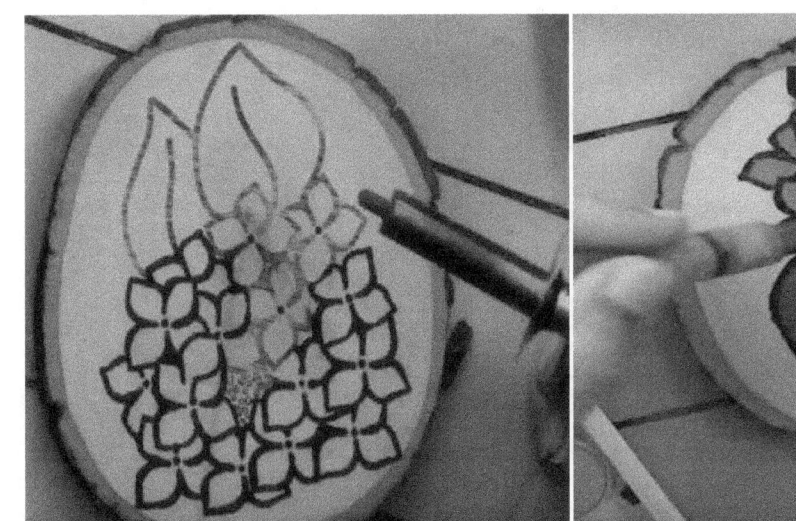
Completing the wood-burning

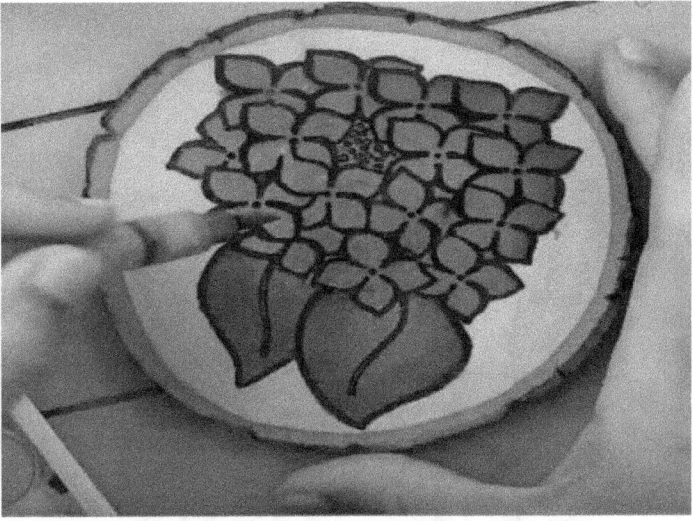
Applying color on the picture

Final coaster after leaving the color to dry for an hour

6. Wooden Tic-Tac-Toe Board

Materials Required

- 1 piece 7" x 10" rectangular or 10" round birch cutting board
- 9 items 2" round timber, regarding 1/2 inch thick, use square details if you desire
- Calligraphy tip or global tip
- Shielding tip
- Gel paints, optional
- Pencil and ruler
- Lacquer or shellac
- Gray-and-white eraser
- Olive oil

Instructions:

- Sand or clean the chopping board. You can find them in the cookware division.
- Using your ruler, split the cutting board into four equal components. From the center point, step 1.5" inch above and below the point. Mark it. Use it as a guide to draw two 10" horizontal lines.
- From the center, draw 1.5 on each side. Use this overview to draw two 10" vertical lines. Make sure that each box should a minimum of have 3" boundary.
- Utilizing the calligraphy point, trace each line using the broadside. Repeat to darken the edges.
- Remove all the pencil traces as well as clean the board with a soft dry fabric. Sand it, if essential.
- Utilizing a fine-grained brush, apply shellac or lacquer on the board. Allow drying completely.
- For the chips, begin with sanding off all the sides of the chip. Using a pre-made layout of "x" and "o," trace it on the timber. Your marks must at least be 1" large. Burn the marks with the calligraphy or universal tip. Make 3 items of each mark.
- To include style to your chips, change to the shading tip as well as use shading on the edge of your chips. You can likewise color only one sort of mark to offer a unique look from the various others.
- Erase all the traces of the pencil.
- Brush olive oil on the chips. Dry it off. Use it with the tic-tac-toe board.

Tic Toe board wooden

7. Easter Eggs

Use these eggs to embellish your house throughout Easter Sunday, or you can use them as regular floor décor.

Drawing design on the egg using a burning tip

Materials Required:

- Unfinished durable egg-shaped wood with level bottoms (available in woodcraft stores)
- Sandpaper
- Woodburner tips
- Gel paints
- Mineral oil
- Non-fusible interfacing
- Graphite paper
- Pencil Eraser

Coloring

Instructions:
- Sand the egg until it becomes smooth. Wipe with a soft towel.
- Publish as well as to enlarge any of the layouts below and trace it to your egg utilizing the interfacing and graphite paper. If it's difficult to make the continual design, you can draw your templates, such as necessary flowers or geometric styles, and attach them with wavy lines.
- Shed the details of the form, making use of the tiny round tip or any proper illustration tip.
- Eliminate the remaining traces of the graphite paper and wipe your egg with the tidy, soft fabric.
- Use the gel paint carefully and also slowly. Begin with the light layer to stay clear of any trickling of color. You may need to make your egg lie down as you use it. It's helpful if you dried out the gel paint for a while before you can transform the egg and repaint the opposite side. This might take a while, relying on the layout you picked and also the size of your egg. You can make use of wax shade pencil instead, but it may not offer you a sharp appearance.
- Dry the egg for a minimum of 5 hours before spraying with oil, lacquer, or shellac.

8. Wooden Key Ring/Key chain

Materials Required:

- Wood Piece
- Sandpaper
- Woodburner
- Gel paints
- Mineral oil
- Non-fusible interfacing
- Graphite paper
- Pencil Eraser

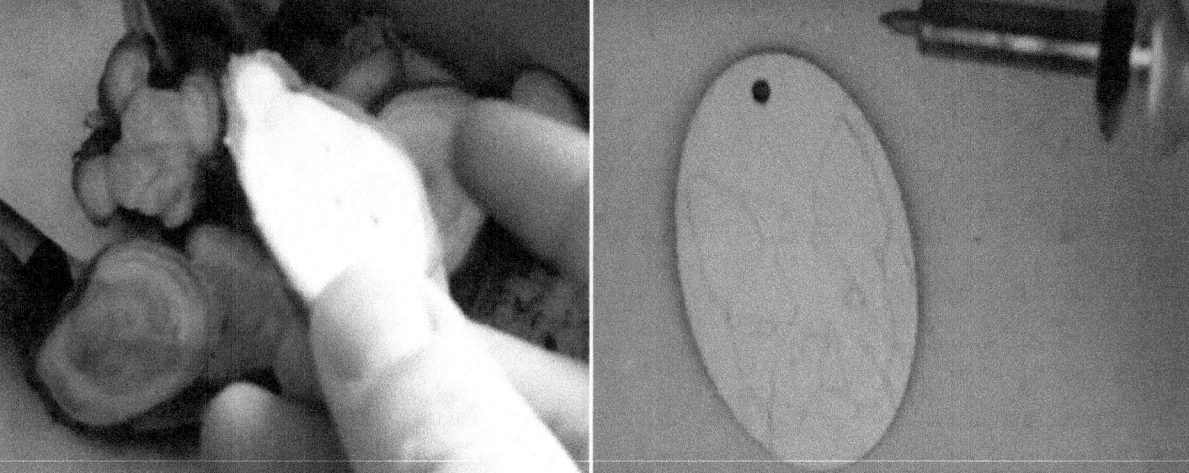

Finding the perfect wood piece | Transferring the pattern

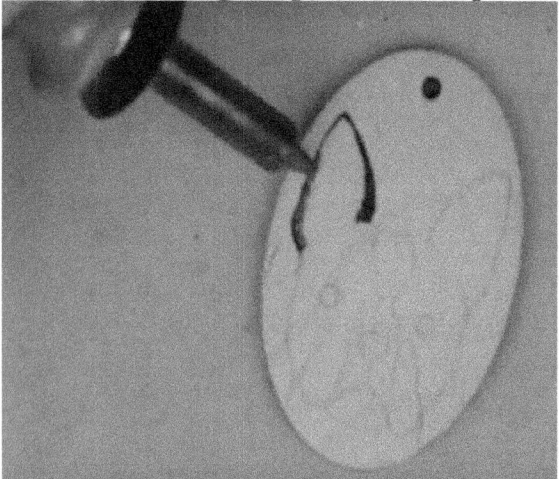

Start burning with edges

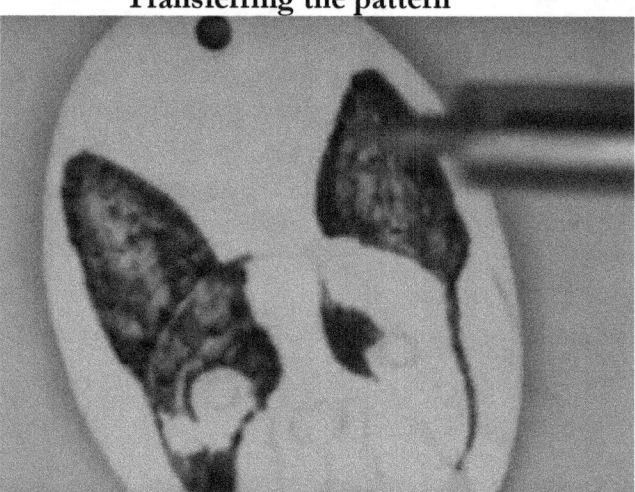

Shade the picture

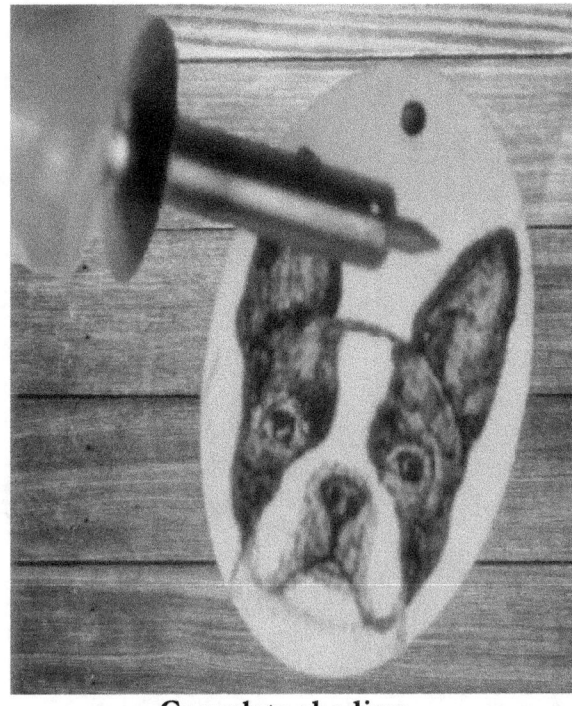

Complete shading   **Put the keyring**

Instructions :

- Sand the timber piece. You can acquire these circular or other shaped blocks at crafts stores.
- Draw the pattern/drawing on your I-pad/Laptop and take the printout from the laser printer.
- Put the design printout face down on the piece of wood and start transferring the image using a wood burner
- Change the Tip and start running the pen on the image transferred on the wood.
- Change the tip and do the shading as per the design.
- Puncture the hole at the top and insert the key chain, as shown above.

9. Leather Key Ring/Key chain (Leather Burning example)

Materials Required:

- Leather Piece
- Sandpaper
- burner
- Mineral oil
- Non-fusible interfacing

- Graphite paper
- Pencil and Eraser

Instructions :

- Transfer design patterns making use of graphite transfer paper. Carbon paper leaves a mark, so use graphite paper.

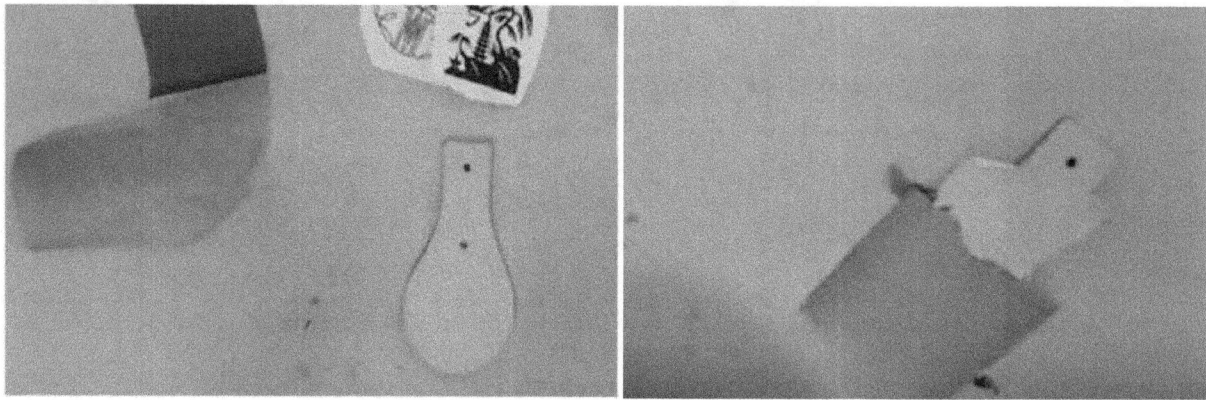

Keep the required material and tape the graphite paper on the leather

- Currently, tape the graphite transfer paper first and after that attempt to tape the pattern. Be careful when you're taping your pattern down as well as not taping on the pattern because that makes it harder to obtain a great transfer.

- Now we draw the pattern off as well as finish it up with a pencil. We use a pencil specifically on leather due to the fact that it's soft. You wish to ensure to sort of move the pencil over the top of the leather instead of pressing it in as you'd certainly theoretically.

- You wish to be mindful below where your pattern goes all the way bent on edge not to tape over because that makes it extremely hard to transfer with your pen.

- Do the basic details; in fact, I don't even do the outdoors border on the graphite paper. You can do that with a pencil later on. Now begin burning the basic overview. You'd be making use of straight for summary as well as cone pointer for filler. You intend to find your place that you're comfortable with on the table you want to relax your arm and also wrist on the table because that makes it steadier.

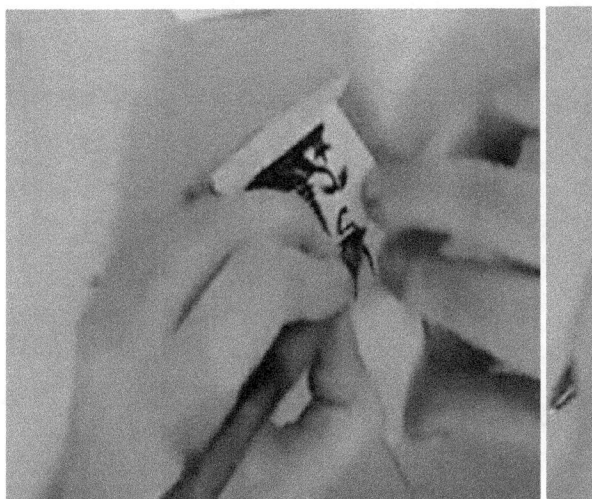 

Run the pencil on the patterns   **Take out the tape and pattern paper**

- Currently, with leather, there are a couple of things that are different than burning timber.
- To begin with, it produces a whole lot more carbon. Be sure to clean your tip twice as usual as you would if you were burning on timber. You must also make sure not to put stress on the leather since you don't intend to gouge it. In contrast, keep in mind time is what makes the dark mark, not stress.

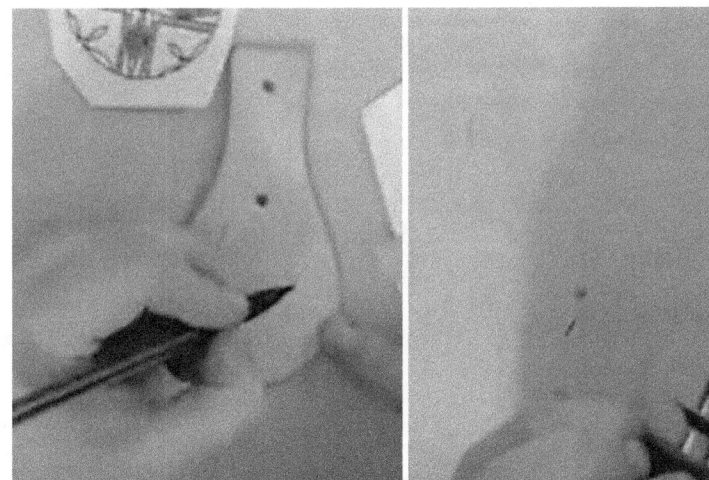 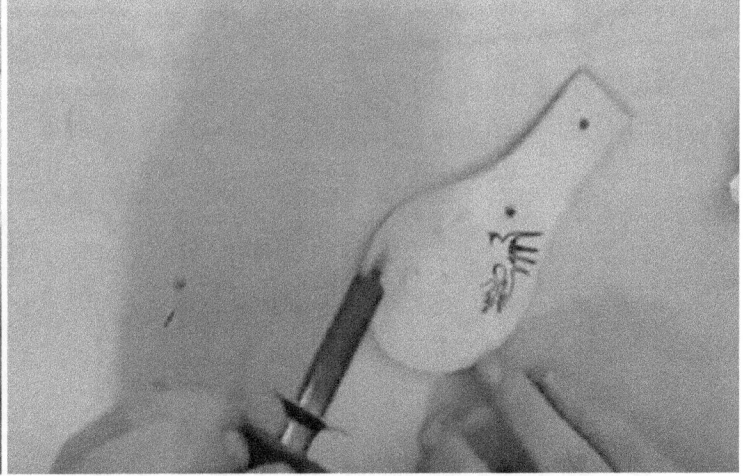

Draw the missing part with pencil again   **Start burning the outlines**

- Kindly fill out the remainder pattern according to the advice provided above. So when you add these finer lines, you're actually turning the wood-burning tool to where the extra narrow part of the tip is, as well as also letting the carbon build up a lot more. In turn, when you include the details in the carbon accumulation, it actually aids because it doesn't make such a thick line.

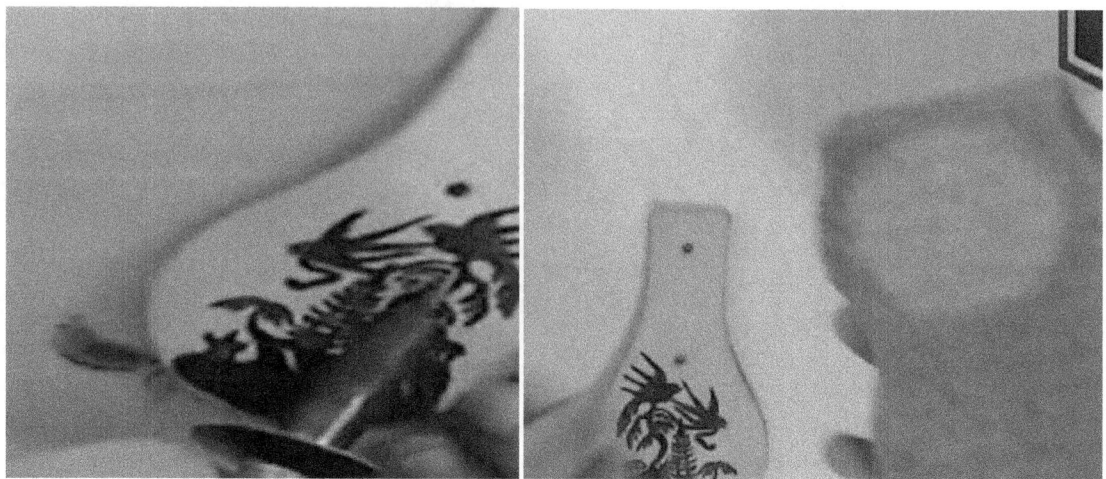

Shading   **Polishing and Finishing**

- Currently switch to the cone tip as well as fill in black as you'd do on timber, except take caution not to place any kind of stress on it as well as you clean your tip often.

- Be sure that your arm remains in a risk-free neutral placement, so you don't stress your wrist or strain your arm; you can see the carbon accumulation on these sandpaper blocks.

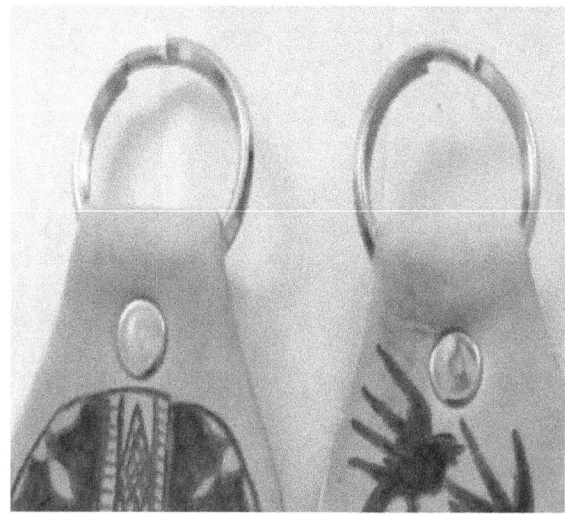

Keychain assembled

- Now include some finishing touches. Use the cone filler once or twice, and if you take your time anywhere and you're likely to rush all over else, so be sure to take your time on the outline because the overview is crucial to how your final product will look.

- If you need to transform the pattern as well, please do that, keeping in mind the essential point. Do not put excessive stress as it gouges the leather.

- You can utilize extreme sheen. You can also put a thin layer and let it completely dry and then put one more layer.

- Bear in mind if you don't want the leather to darken, you have to reduce the number of layers that you place on. If you desire it darker, you can place much more coats on since it darkens the leather.

10. Wooden Spoon

Materials Required:

- Wooden Spoon
- Sandpaper
- Woodburner
- Gel paints
- Mineral oil
- Non-fusible interfacing
- Graphite paper
- Pencil Eraser

Instructions

- Take a printout of the pattern or letter to be transferred (** Use a printout of mirror letter images!)
- Using graphite paper and transferring tip, transfer the image
- Burn the transferred image or letter by the regular tp, as shown

Spoon and Woodeburner(Walnut Hollow Model)

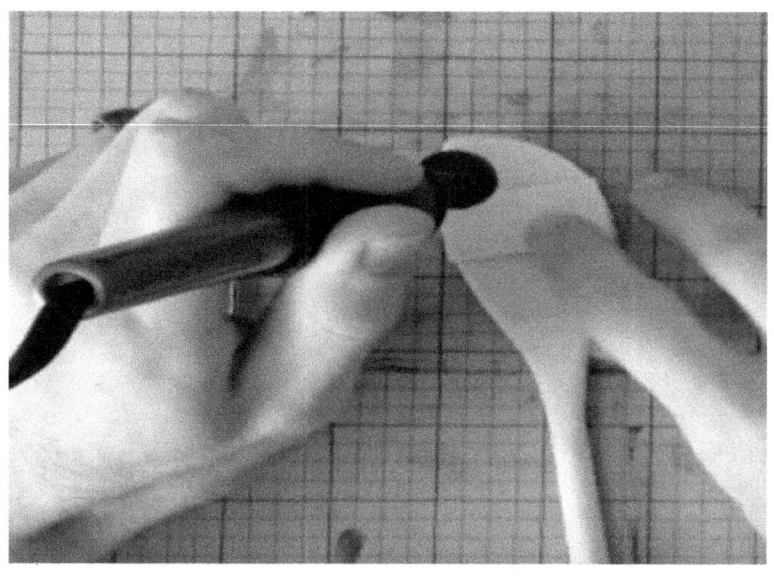

Transferring patterns or letters

You can also draw several patterns on the spoon, as shown below:

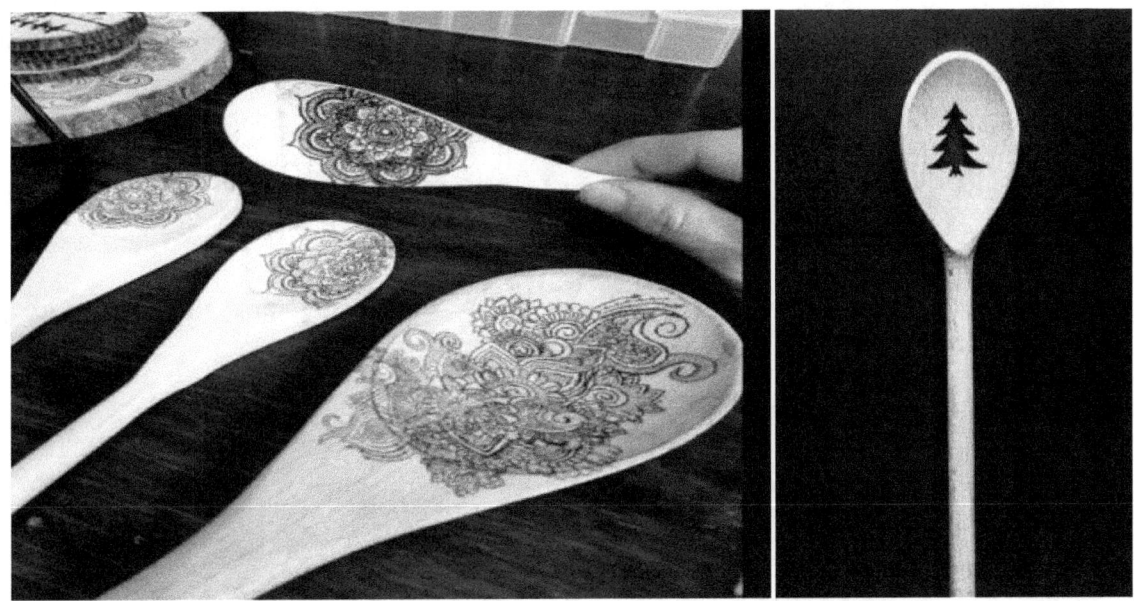

Mandala Designs **Christmas Spoon**

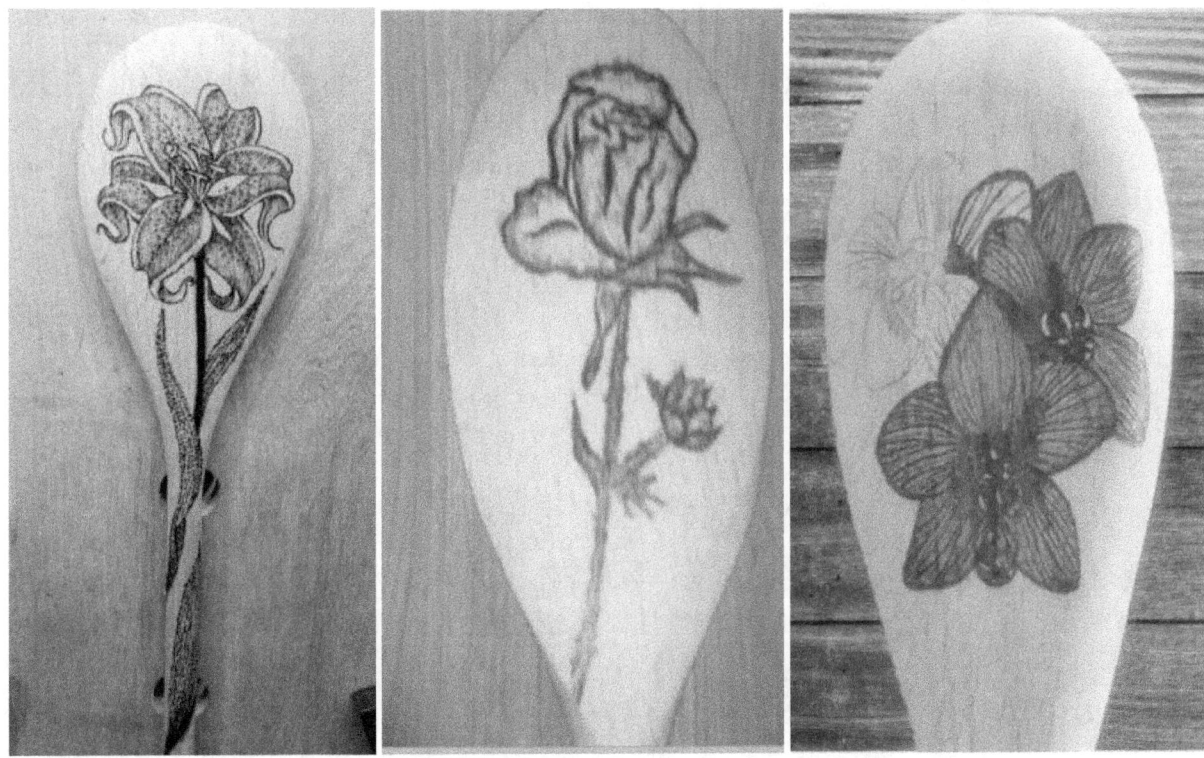

Flower Designs

7. FAQ's of practitioners

During my journey into pyrography, I interacted with many practitioners who were wood & leather crafters. We had many discussions around techniques and best practices. I've maintained a notebook to jot down the essential points to remember for future reference. I'm providing a few of those points in FAQ format with examples and pictures wherever necessary. These questions are from all the topics in Pyrography and aren't listed in a particular sequence.

1. **Look at the work below to determine how to enhance it and make it more three dimensional (3D):**

Shadows and also highlights are what includes depth. The containers are cylindrical, so you can seek out just how to shade different forms to assist on those. The wheel spokes are likewise cylindrical, so they'll adhere to the same guidelines for shading. I always require a recommendation image to work from, however knowing the guidelines for how you shade different forms is valuable.

2. **What's a live edge?**

The natural wood, whose edges are unfinished, is called a live edge. Few people opt for live edges for making realistic sceneries — an example of live wood is depicted below.

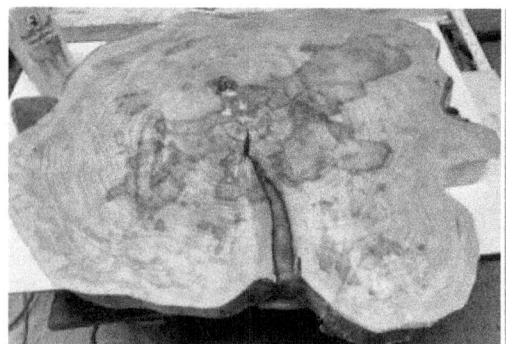

3. **For those of you who don't consider yourself very artistic, how do you get your images?**

   There are no real shortcuts to drawing your designs. You can do things like find (free) photos you like, and digitally, draw on a layer over them, so you can sketch form without having to know correct proportions. This can help a lot.

   And with practice, drawing does get easier. If you have an iPad, you can get drawing pens for it, too.

   Rapidresizer.com: You can upload images and turn them into stencils on this website. Yes, you can also create a letter stencils. It only costs money if you want special options, but you'll able to do without those options.

4. **How do you get your images?**

   When you look for a subject on google search, add "free" in front of the item (cat, dog, elephant, fox) line art, silhouette, coloring pages, vector, clip art, etc.

5. **Is there some arty app/website for getting artistic fonts?**

   There are many sites you can refer to accordingly. One of them is dafont.com.
   It offers many free use fonts. I size and reverse them in the computer, then print from the laser ink printer, then heat transfer to the wood. The process works great with lettering as well as basic outlines and silhouettes, but not portraits - you don't want hard lines in pictures.

6. **Optima vs. Razertip (burner comparison): A perspective of my fellow burner who has used both over the years**

The best response I can give you is Optima is less expensive than a razer tip for about the same top quality. I use to have a razer tip that does not work so well; however, lots of individuals like their razer tip. Optima is about $100 much less, and the pens are cheaper. The capacity to re-coat your tips for $8 instead of getting a whole brand-new pen after the chromium oxide disappears is an incentive too. I don't recognize if razer tip pens have an oxide layer or otherwise, but the Optima pens hold heat consistently (Note: This is one user's experience).

7. **Which oils are safe to use on cutting boards?**

    Safe and recommended:
    - Mineral oil
    - Bee wax
    - Coconut oil
    - Carnauba
    - Baking soda
    - Lemon juice

8. **Can I burn on bamboo cutting boards or utensils?**

The answer is; indeed, you can. But it can be a threat, and I'll certainly clarify a lot more soon. You'll likely want to pre-sand your bamboo with a fine-grit sandpaper. Not only for surface area texture conditioning like a regular shed surface area, however additionally in case a sealant was used on the surface to avoid chemical fumes.

Now some words of cautioning about bamboo. It's an all-natural composite of cellulose fibers.

A lot of people aren't aware that bamboo is not timber. Wood comes from trees and also usually has a lot of tough fibers and structural cells in its make-up.

Bamboo is the world's tallest grass from the Poaceae family members. (Refer: https://en.wikipedia.org/wiki/Bamboo)

Unlike wood, bamboo fibers have lignin. To make these right into tools, fibers are often pulled apart, soaked in water, dried, compressed back along with adhesives or chemical bonding agents.

It's always a good tip to find out if that holds with your item and also to make use of excellent ventilation from a solid fan.

Additionally, as a result of the lignin density in bamboo fibers, it requires to be well sanded and also requires a lower heat level as it has a low burning point temperature when compared to wood.

9. I'm allergic to basswood. What kind of wood that burns the same way?

Other options

- Poplar
- Veg Tanned Leather
- Water Color Paper

10. My wood burner pen is breaking more often?

If you're breaking your pens, I think you must be pushing way too hard. The trick is Low heat, light touch, and burning over the same spot until it's the desired color. If your tips are really hot, they'll break. Moderate temperatures are the key.

11. While transferring pictures on wood, do you transfer the only outline or also transfer details?

When I map the picture onto the board (making use of graphite paper), I see to it I get the outline vividly. I attempt to obtain several of the major shaded areas marked by scribbling on that particular location. I don't stress too much regarding smaller, shaded locations. When I burn, I keep the initial picture alongside me for reference to make sure I'm shading the right areas.

12. I've been holding onto one of my pieces in the same place and have almost dirty hand marks. How to get rid of those hand marks?

It's a best practice to have a clean sheet of paper under your hand to cover the part you have not burnt. And relocate around as you are dealing with your image. This saves you from smearing the graphite and tidy hands.

Glassine works. It's a thin paper that doesn't grab anything. It looks similar to tracing paper but isn't. You can see thru it, making it much easier to line points up. Denatured alcohol is likewise risk-free to utilize. It dries rapidly and also does not increase the grain. A small bit on a cotton rag ought to take any dust off. I use it to wipe down my burnings before adding different colors and sealing.

Get it off using an eraser or maybe a light sanding. Nevertheless, something I've found is that no matter how tidy our hands are, they do transfer natural oils from skin to the wood. I believe its probably the oils that are making the discoloration.

13. **Many individuals burn purchased wood items like guitars and also slicing boards, yet how do you know if they've been treated with something that shouldn't be burned?**

You mentioned guitars and cutting boards. So I'll just address those products. Wooden cutting boards, unless otherwise defined, are constantly treated with a sealer at minimum. Some are discolored or treated with chemical fungal retardants.

A built guitar is also constantly treated and also secured. Nevertheless, several companies supply guitar packages and guitar blanks. These are untreated to allow paint, staining, and artwork, prior to securing the finished product. The majority of burners choose these types of wood for burning.

14. **Which is the best wood to start your journey in pyrography?**

Basswood as its soft and light-colored. It takes your time, so have patience. Also, try and start light and burn darker as you need to.

15. **How do I get rid of a dent on the wood caused due to heavy tracing or just a tool dropped on it?**

Using a damp paper towel, wipe it over the damage, press with hot iron simply sufficient to let some heavy steam right into the surface, don't burn the paper towel. Allow it completely dry. Be happy to see the wood fibers go back to their pre-crushed status!

16. **What are the different options to color the design?**

- The watercolor pencil is the easiest for me to use, but you can water down acrylics
- Alcohol markers. Sharpies. Put a thin coat of lacquer on first, and it stops the bleeding into the wood. Be careful with red as it may bleed into the next coat of lacquer
- I used Prismacolor pencils.
- Watercolor is good, but be careful since some wood absorbs water, and it can run over the borders where you want your color to be.
- You can use Gouache, which is a paint that acts like a watercolor but can be dark/bright like an acrylic. It depends on the amount of water you use.

17. **If you're going to purchase a laser printer to help make an image transferring faster, can you check out different printers on-site?**
    - laser

- **inkjet laser**
- **monochrome**
- **color**

Not an inkjet printer. Laserjet printer is what you desire. Inkjet is simply that: it's ink and also doesn't transfer well. The laser makes use of a printer toner powder cartridge and heat.

So when you publish, the paper will be cozy. Make sure you mirror the print or at least on the computer to turn your print. Otherwise, your picture will certainly be backward, or your letters will undoubtedly be backward when you transfer. Use an iron on the back of the paper when it's laid on the board.

The heat will certainly transfer the heated ink toner on wood. Big tip: make sure the wood is sanded extremely smooth.

18. What are the different methods to transmit images to wood than the old carbon paper and also to map everything?

Try to stay clear of carbon paper; it's very hard to remove any remaining marks. Either utilize graphite transfer paper (Saral or Tracedown are the most effective or scribble around the back of your picture with a soft (3 or 4B) pencil.

19. What are the different nibs used for shading? Can you give me a few opinions?

You can utilize a spear shader. Mainly an 18m tool optima. It will do great for both dark and light shades. You can use it for drawing contours as well as mixing.

You can also use a ball pointer to get textures and even heat or scribble slower to obtain darker shade.

I must admit my inclination towards using the spoon tip as it feels much more natural. I never found anything better for shading than the calligraphy tip. My second favorite is the universal tip.

20. What are your experiences of burning on Olivewood?

The best way for olivewood is to burn, sand, burn, sand, and keep repeating it. Olive wood is oily as well as, so it burns at various rates, depending on the shade in the grain. We've learned to stay away from the lighter locations and also determined designs that are free of charge to the wood.

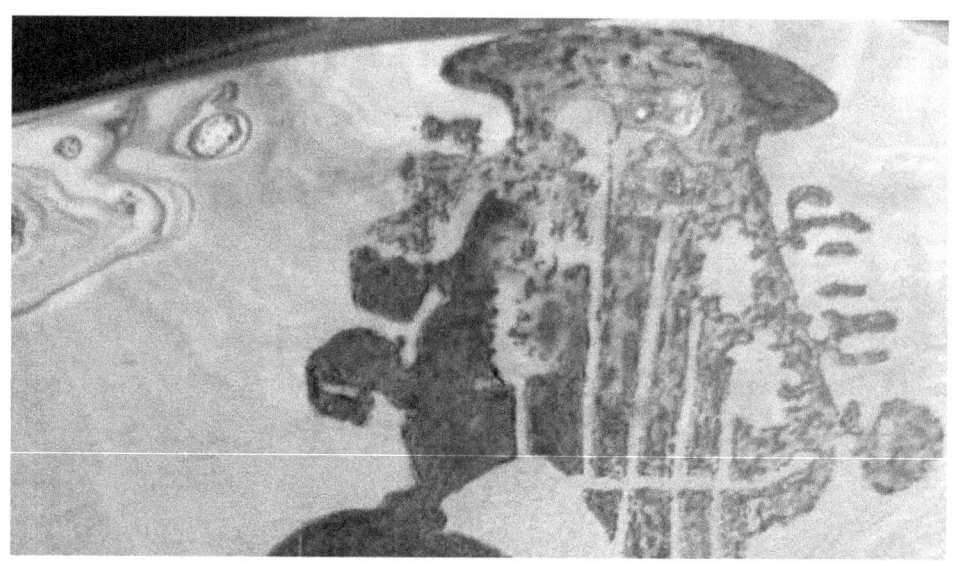

Burning on Olivewood

8. Several Sample Designs &Patterns for Pyrography

1. Indian Mandala Design

2. Fox Design

3. Tiger Mascot

4. Dragon Design

5. Koala Design

6. Butterfly Design

7. Owl Design

Conclusion

The option of writing with fire has always fascinated humans.

The art of Pyrography has existed for centuries. The beauty is that it has been modified over these years.

I started it for merely making a nameplate, which then evolved into writing quotes and finally complex pictures.

Each practitioner has a similar journey, but I suggest aligning the theme you're drawing to near to your heart or something you really like.

One of my colleagues is passionate about a space-related theme, and he's creating an impressive, detailed artwork. Another one was interested in bikes and engines, so he specialized in burning motorbike-related pictures.

Another point involves taking proactive care of your health and following safety measures. This is very important as this art consists of heat and irritation related issues. A few basic precautions pertain to always remembering to wear gloves and masks, work in an open and well-ventilated area, and use some fume /smoke extractor. In case of any irritation, immediately consult a professional.

Wishing you all the best for your first project!

Cheers,

Stephen Fleming

(If you liked the book, kindly leave a review. In case you want to offer a suggestion or share something, kindly email valueadd2life@gmail.com.)

www.ingramcontent.com/pod-product-compliance
Lightning Source LLC
LaVergne TN
LVHW081528060526
838200LV00045B/2038